Israel
Observed

Translated from the French by Jean Joss

Victor Malka

KAYE & WARD · LONDON

OXFORD UNIVERSITY PRESS · NEW YORK

Contents

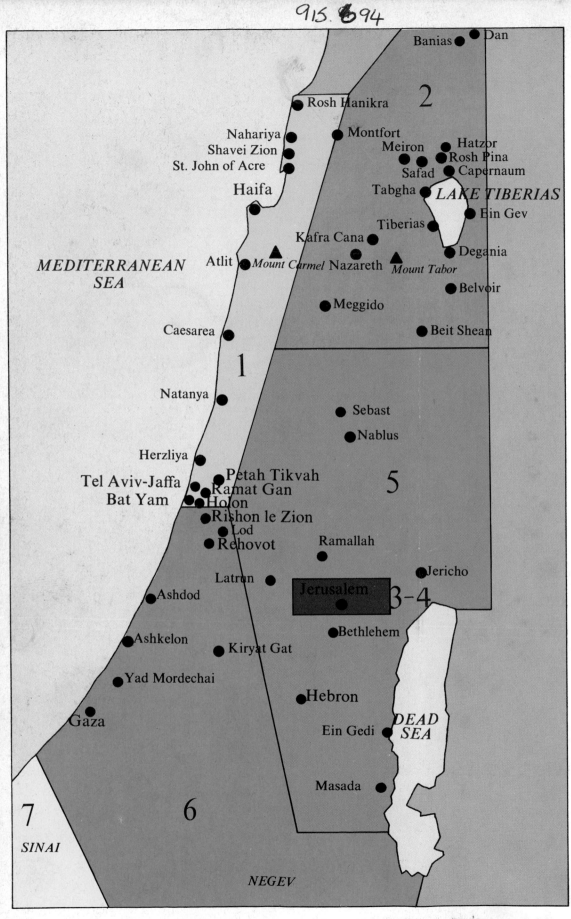

Banias · Dan

2

Rosh Hanikra
Nahariya
Montfort
Shavei Zion
Meiron · Hatzor
St. John of Acre
Rosh Pina
Safad · Capernaum
Haifa
Tabgha · *LAKE TIBERIAS*
Ein Gev
Kafra Cana · Tiberias
▲
Atlit · *Mount Carmel* Nazareth ▲ Degania
Mount Tabor
Belvoir

Meggido

*MEDITERRANEAN
SEA*

Caesarea

1

Beit Shean

Natanya

Sebast

Nablus

Herzliya

Petah Tikvah
Tel Aviv-Jaffa
Ramat Gan
Bat Yam
Holon
5
Rishon le Zion
Lod
Rehovot
Ramallah

Latrun · Jericho

Ashdod
Jerusalem 3-4

Bethlehem

Ashkelon
Kiryat Gat

Yad Mordechai
Hebron

*DEAD
SEA*
Gaza
Ein Gedi

Masada

7
6
SINAI
NEGEV

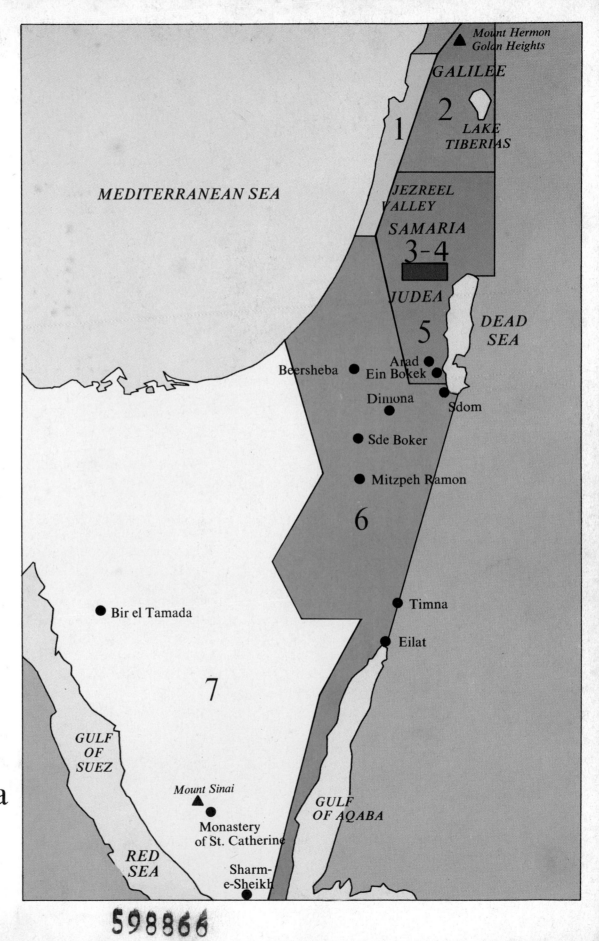

MEDITERRANEAN SEA

Mount Hermon
Golan Heights

GALILEE

1

2

LAKE
TIBERIAS

JEZREEL
VALLEY

SAMARIA

3-4

JUDEA

5

DEAD
SEA

Beersheba • Arad
Ein Bokek •
Dimona • Sdom

• Sde Boker

• Mitzpeh Ramon

6

• Bir el Tamada

• Timna

• Eilat

7

GULF
OF
SUEZ

Mount Sinai
▲ •
Monastery
of St. Catherine

GULF
OF AQABA

RED
SEA

Sharm-
e-Sheikh •

6
The Negev
and the Red Sea

7
Sinai

1

Tel Aviv and the North Coast

'And I will bring again the captivity of my people of Israel, and they shall build the waste cities and inhabit them and they shall plant vineyards and drink the wine thereof; they shall also make gardens and eat the fruit of them.'

Amos IX, 14

From the moment you set foot in this country you are confronted by two different worlds. Israel, a land of contrasts and paradoxes, is a planet in miniature, a microcosm of peoples. Its inhabitants have come from all corners of the world. The policeman who stamps your passport is obviously Moroccan. Although his accent betrays his country of origin he regards himself as an Israeli. A little further on, the customs official is perhaps Rumanian or Bulgarian. You can speak whatever language you like, there will always be someone who can understand you.

But first of all the tourist becomes a pilgrim and reverently caresses the dirty oil-stained asphalt, kissing the ground of the Holy Land. This ritual has become part of the daily scene, no longer evoking surprise. You too should take part in it all and absorb all the mixed impressions which you will receive from the initial contact with this simultaneously solemn and joyful country.

For a time as he approaches **Tel Aviv** the traveller can enjoy the traditional pleasures of tourism. Coming in to land at Lod (or Lydda), the Boeing banks round the gently sweeping curve of the coast. **The seafront** spreads out proudly below, dotted with several sky-scrapers suggesting a small-scale Manhattan.

Tel Aviv . . . the name itself is evocative. It means 'hill of the springtime'. It was at Tel Aviv that the independent state of Israel was proclaimed on Friday, the eve of the Sabbath, May 14th, 1948. It was, perforce, a hasty declaration – at the same time the country was preparing for the first war against the Arab countries.

This city has neither Jerusalem's gravity nor the mysterious undertones of Haifa. The stones here do not evoke the spirit of past centuries as they do elsewhere. There are certainly a few tombs dating from the bronze age which were discovered at Tel Quasileh and Djerisheh, and also the fortifications built by Alexander Jannaeus excavated along the river Yarqon, but none of these could confer upon Tel Aviv the prestige of a city which has History indelibly stamped upon it.

Born yesterday, this city already has half a million inhabitants and, stretching irresistibly towards tomorrow, it is preparing to double its population.

Tel Aviv – the seafront

Tel Aviv is a white city, without charm and has nothing to offer the tourist that cannot be seen in any European capital. But beauty and harmony of architecture created from centuries of enduring and striving are luxuries reserved for older nations. The young nations can with their new cities offer nothing but the enthusiasm with which they are built.

Tel Aviv, conceived by architects nostalgic for their European origins, was meant to be the 'anti-ghetto' city – this it most certainly is. The cruel judgement of a Jewish philosopher condemns it remorselessly: 'The beginnings of the Diaspora are in Tel Aviv.'

In 1909 the members of an association of haloutzim (pioneers) acquired several of the dunes at the entrance to Jaffa. Ottoman law forbade them from owning even the smallest tract of sand but the haloutzim found Dutch nominees to act for them. And what was in the beginning a mere suburb of Jaffa, became Tel Aviv, now the country's most important city. From then on both have formed a single municipality.

Jaffa (Joppa of the New Testament) was according to legend built by Japhet, son of Noah. Its Hebrew name, Yafo, means 'the beautiful'. A few houses still remain from its splendid antiquity but they conjure up more a style of decoration than a city.

It was at Jaffa that Jonah set sail for distant Tarsis and it was on this shore that the whale threw him back. Its port was conquered by the Pharoah Tuthmosis III who had his name carved here. And it was in Jaffa that the Greeks placed the legend of Andromeda, daughter of the king of Ethiopia.

Myths abound here where civilisations co-exist.

Aerial view of Jaffa and Tel Aviv

Kebab seller

Today Jaffa is dedicated to the more practical pursuit of the 'unrestrained delights' of the Tel Aviv pleasure quarters. Here there are art galleries, artists' workshops and **terrace-cafés** overlooking the sea. A visit to Tel Aviv is not complete without an evening devoted to 'Jaffa by night'. Avant-garde artists and venerable Yemenite artisans live happily here together with (if one dare mention them) streetwalkers and down-and-outs. One of the quarters of Jaffa is now called 'Little Montmartre'. In the shabby eating houses at the foot of the hill you can sit among the ceaseless players of dominoes or backgammon, a glass of *arac* (that insidious drink!) or failing that, a harmless *mits echko-liyot* (grapefruit juice) on the table in

Yemenite jeweller

front of you and try a kebab from this lazy, rowdy, good-natured city.

Chants emanate from the Arab divas, pungent fumes rise from the kebabs and *shishliks*, idle gossip

Jaffa – a terrace-café

drones on late into the night, all inducing a certain sense of well-being. These pleasures are momentary, embraced with consummate skill by those who are not concerned with searching for the sense in life but rather with celebrating in their own inimitable fashion the life of the senses.

9

Night falls swiftly, almost without warning. From Jaffa to **Tel Aviv** the coast road comes alive with the lights of discotheques and nightclubs. In the evening the hardworking population of the city enjoys a more oriental tempo of life, indulging in the pleasant pastime of idleness and above all enjoying the unceasing pleasure of impassioned debate. The atmosphere is reminiscent of a 'paseo' in a middle-eastern 'Seville'.

Nightlife is centred on **Dizengoff Street** which is the traditional evening meeting place for young and old alike. It is Tel Aviv's answer to both London's Piccadilly and Greenwich Village, New York. An open rivalry exists between the two most famous cafés in the street, the Rowal and its neighbour the Kassit. Each has its own class of customer and every Tel Avivian frequents the one with which he feels the most affinity. 'High society' people go to the Rowal in order to

be seen in public and you can often find politicians there relaxing in shirt-sleeves. The Kassit on the other hand is the domain of the bohemian and intellectual elements in Tel Aviv society. Not long ago it was the daily haunt of such well-known literary figures as national poets Alterman and Shlonsky. Today it has become a haven for satirical hack writers, aspiring artists and the inevitable hippies who have somehow got stranded here on their way to Katmandu. In the Kassit petitions are formulated and lampoons composed to appear in the next day's newspapers. Here, too, the Israeli sense of humour is given free rein at the expense of the establishment and prominent political figures.

In spite of the ever present threat of war, Israel is a country where gaiety is always much in evidence. Occasionally you are reminded of the infamous concentration camps of a quarter of a century ago by the sight of a scar on a

Young Israeli girl

Tel Aviv – the Kassit café

Dizengoff Street

11

Tel Aviv – the carnival for the festival of Purim

bare arm glimpsed in the street. The memory of this tragedy is kept alive in the nation's collective consciousness. It is not something that can easily be forgotten and sometimes a man's laughter takes on a brittle note as he remembers the depth of despair his people once experienced . . .

The new generation has grown up far away from the rigours of exile and without the pervading fear instilled in their forebears. For these sabarim genocide on such a scale has an air of mystery. It is incredible, yet nonetheless true. They have to make themselves imagine it so that they can hand down the memory to future generations. But they themselves are proud to have come to maturity under an Israeli sky. They have never learnt the art of humble submission. They are realists who know they can count only on themselves. As Hillel would put it, 'If I don't believe in myself, who will believe in me?' They are pragmatists too and disapprove of the elders' voluntarily circumscribed lifestyle. They despise the traditional Jewish shibboleths which have provided their parents with a refuge for so long. The French philosopher Georges Friedmann described this younger generation as 'having lost many of their parents' faults which stemmed from the ghettos but also many of the good qualities engendered there.'

Certainly the two generations have little if anything in common. The new generation has been moulded in a fierce beauty, forged by self-assurance and energy. There is now no trace of fear and old Jewish complexes and anguishes have vanished. Their gaze is unflinching, their handshake firm. The new language is direct and without embellishments, their sense of humour corrosive. Israeli culture today is drawn from the whole of the Bible. The festivals celebrated are in honour of the heroic figures in the Torah. A few more ancient celebrations have been secularised. One such is **Purim,** commemorating the miraculous escape, as a result of Queen Esther's intervention, of Jews in the Persian Empire from a pogrom in Babylon. Today this has become an excuse for a colourful **Tel Aviv street carnival** which continues long after the children are in bed and asleep.

Although the new Israeli culture thrives on European values as well as those nurtured at home by Israel's 'new society', the essential age-old threads of Judaism have not disappeared from today's lifestyle. There is a permanent consciousness of Jewish history and a pervading sense of their deep links with the Diaspora. From the cradle the young Israelis are aware that their new nation has not been created from scratch but is founded on a storehouse of collective Jewish memory extending way back through the centuries. The state's

The star of David and the seven-branched candelabra – a game in the sand

emblems the six-pointed **Star of David** and the **seven-branched candelabra** from the Temple at Jerusalem, were not adopted by chance, even though they may now be found traced in the sand like a child's doodles. The menorah burning with its eternal flame has always symbolised the hope of Israel's resurrection ever since the Temple was destroyed so far back in Jewish history.

From Tel Aviv, a future metropolis already devouring its suburbs, the motorway climbs northwards along the coast. You soon pass through Natanya, a sensual little city almost entirely devoted to the tourist trade. It is full of luxury hotels and holiday clubs and is particularly rich in cafés and terraces where you can rediscover an atmosphere of joviality and abundant gossip among the refugees from the former French Algeria who have come here in great numbers seeking another niche in the sunshine.

The important village Or Akiva heralds the approach of **Caesarea**. Its name means 'light of Akiva' and is a reminder that it was at Caesarea the Romans murdered the holy Rabbi Akiva. Master among the masters, the glory and splendour of the Torah, he was the defender of the cause of Bar Kokhba whose revolt against the Roman occupation eventually foundered with the fall of

Caesarea – the Roman aquaduct

Massada in the year 135.

The city was built by Herod the Great around the ancient citadel of Strato's Tower. The sycophantic Herod named it Caesarea and openly dedicated it to Caesar Augustus. It grew quickly into 'Caesarea in Palestine' the bridgehead for the Roman Empire's military imperialism. The members of the neighbouring kibbutz of Sdot-Yam have excavated the ruins of the swimming pool, the hippodrome and a superb amphitheatre 95 metres long and 62 metres wide. It is in this amphitheatre where today an annual classical music festival takes place that once long ago Jews were thrown to wild beasts after an unsuccessful revolt against the procurator Gessius Florus in 66 BC.

An **aquaduct** five and a half miles in length, its arches still engulfed in sand, bears witness to the Roman talent for exploiting occupied countries. The Talmud recounts a conversation between a sage and common man who marvels at the civilising achievements of Rome. The doctor of law avers that 'these baths, aquaducts and circuses were constructed for their fat public officials and prostitutes, not for the ordinary people'.

Caesarea – remains of the Roman port

In 1101 the Crusaders took possession of Caesarea and Baldwin the First discovered a vase encrusted with diamonds there, the Holy Grail of Celtic legend which was henceforth put on display in Genoa cathedral. Saint Louis arrived here in 1252 and had the surrounding defensive walls built. The Sultan Baibars utterly destroyed the city in 1265.

Excavations started at Caesarea only some 20 years ago have revealed **traces** of an extraordinarily rich archaeological heritage.

We rejoin the road to the north the ultimate point on which is **Rosh Hanikra**. The first foothills of Mount Carmel with its violet mass capped in pines and cypresses stands out on the horizon. At this sight you, like Chateaubriand, author of *L'Itineraire de Paris a Jerusalem*, can also experience the impression of a moment which is 'at once something religious and majestic'.

Carmel, the sacred mountain for the three great religions, crowns the city of Haifa with gardens and forests. The Song of Songs, which the doctors of the Jewish law regard as more than just a wonderful love song, has King Solomon describing the Shulamite woman, saying 'Thine head upon thee is like Carmel', while the prophet Isaiah sings of its brilliance and splendour.

It was on this mystical mountain, like no other, that Elijah defied the prophets

The bay of Haifa and the Bahaist temple

of Baal. Tradition has it that it was on Carmel, too, that Pythagorus sought refuge for his meditations. Here also is the splendid terraced Persian garden of the **Bahaist temple**, whose golden dome majestically dominates the view of **the bay of Haifa**. Who were these Bahaists who appeared from time to time in various parts of the world? Their doctrine is named for its founder Baha U'liah (glory to God) and it preaches the unity of all faiths, all races and all men for it says 'The Creator is unique'. The Bahaists have neither religious rites, nor preachers, nor creed. They have only this gold and green jewel set on Carmel. Haifa, city of harmony, is their Jerusalem.

City of harmony? Haifa has neither Tel Aviv's artificiality nor the gravity of Jerusalem. It is a genuine city, presenting the same daily face to the tourists as it does to its inhabitants. It is an uncomplicated, hardworking place named 'the red city' and shows reserve, though not timidity. Life here is regulated with the same wisdom

Mediterranean coastline near Rosh Hanikra

The Jezreel Valley

Haifa – a house in the old quarter

found in ancient cities, something that is beginning to slip away from the metropolises of Europe. Hadar Hacarmel, the highest part of the town, is a true model of urbanism where the luxuriant vegetation is respected.

The port is really the city centre. Channelled here is all the produce of the gentle fertile **Jezreel valley**, not long ago a marshy area, today the country's 'storehouse'. As they cultivate it the Israeli peasants must often recall the great battles which took place here. This was where Baraq, urged on by Deborah the prophetess, vanquished the armies of Yabine, King of Hatzor. It was in this valley too that King Saul drew up his troops before the battle of Mount Gilboa where he was killed.

The kibbutznikim have today turned this place of war into a place of peace. They have drained the valley and reworked the countryside.

For a long time the kibbutzim were phalansteries. Those who dwelt in them and accepted the conditions of life there were motivated by a real sense of social justice and brotherhood. They were secularised versions of the Jewish 'prophets' in a guise more suited to today. They also kept traces of Tolstoyan dreams in their hearts.

Today the kibbutzim are becoming havens of culture where writers, musicians and artists are incubated with as much care as that formerly lavished on the seedlings. The writer Amos Oz has assigned his author's rights to the community of the kibbutz where he was born. In **Kabri, Shami the sculptor** has an enormous studio where he creates his huge works of tortured metal. And his profits too are

Kabri – Shami the sculptor's studio

paid into the general account of his kibbutz.

On the return journey from a trip around the outskirts of Haifa you should not be afraid to go down into the **Arab cafés** in the port. Here Jews and Arabs co-exist peacefully in friendly debate or conspiratorial silence over a glass of *arac* or a Turkish coffee. You should not be surprised to find Jews speaking Arabic and Arabs talking in Hebrew.

Haifa is a city whose inhabitants have peace in their hearts. They do not speak of killing but rather extol friendship and brotherly love. They are partners in work and in leisure.

Haifa, city of quietude.

Samaritans' annual pilgrimage

In the passes of the Carmel range are several village communities teeming with people of a highly original character. They are called **Druze** and, from the eleventh century onwards, they have been dissidents from Islam and have been persecuted as heretics by Muslims. The state of Israel granted them the status of an independent religious community and ever since the 18 villages in Carmel and Galilee where they settled have been integrated into, and loyally taken part in, the life of the country. The Israeli army has every confidence in them since they serve in its most dangerous volunteer units, notwithstanding the fact that fellow members of their religion live in Lebanon or Jebel el Druz in Syria.

Their name could possibly have originated from one of their chiefs who lived in the eighteenth century, Mohammed ben Ismael Eddarogi. Curiously enough the ordinary members of the congregation know little of their religion. The secrets of their devotion are handed down only by the village elders and the sages from father to son. It is perhaps an elitist religion but, even so, the sages and the faithful gather together on 25th April each year at the Horns of Hittin in Galilee for the grand annual pilgrimage to the tomb of Jethro the Midianite, the father-in-law of Moses. It is from him they claim their descent.

The few Druze students at Jerusalem university or the Institute of Technology at Haifa soon make their presence felt. Kamal Mansour, a young deputy in Israel's parliament, the Knesset, explains 'According to our tradition the women of the Druze community stand behind the fighting men during a battle to urge them on. No Druze woman would ever marry a warrior who had fled from the field of battle'. They are active in the economic life of the country as businessmen but mainly as prosperous farmers. It is only natural that their own rich folklore should make an impact on that of the nation as a whole.

Apart from the Druze there are other minorities living in Israel who have the status of independent communities. These are mainly Caraites who number about 12,000 or so. Their movement is founded on denial of the Talmud and the oral tradition and it accepts only the teaching of the Bible which they follow to the letter.

As for the Samaritans, they have a total veneration for the Bible, the book of Joshua in particular. Like the Caraites they completely reject the authority of the Talmud. Today there are not more than a few hundred in the country, 500 in Holon and 200 in Nablus.

The great **annual pilgrimage** takes place on Mount Gerizim near Nablus.

'Ein maavar' (no exit). The northern route stops at **Rosh Hanikra** at the frontier with Lebanon, and you have to retrace your steps. Wandering lazily down the coast you come to Akhziv which belongs to the Club Mediterranean. Not far away a new village has grown up full of long-haired guitar-toting hippies from all over the place. Their master of ceremonies had an ingenious idea to make their fortune. He declared the independence of his domain to the world then took the initiative of celebrating 'hippy marriages' there in front of international photographers. Rather like Father Ubu of Brecht fame transformed into a genial businessman!

Then here is Nahariya, a charming little seaside resort which has become the recognised spot to spend one's honeymoon in Israel. The town was built by German refugees saved from the death camps and it is a model of what in Israel is often scornfully referred to as 'the yekké* spirit'. Its people are obsessed with good order and demonstrate a methodical slowness and ponderous gravity, all of which are considered as virtues in Nahariya.

The port of Saint John of Acre (Akko) gleams in a halo of dazzling light which seems to reflect the towers and city walls of the ancient Ptolemais. In olden times it was coveted by all the great powers who played a role in the Middle East. There is reference to it even 19 centuries before the birth of Christ in letters discovered at Tel el Amarna. The Pharoah Tuthmosis III conquered it in 1450 BC. Since Akko was at the northernmost point of his realm Solomon gave it up to Tyre. Ptolemy I razed it to the ground in 312 BC and another Ptolemy, the second to bear the name, rebuilt it and named it Ptolemais. It was favoured with the status of a Roman colony in 47 AD and was called 'Colonia Claudia Ptolemais'. It was the brotherhood of St. John's Hospital or the Knights of St. John who gave it the name of Saint John of Acre.

Rosh Hanikra

* Yekké is a nickname given to Jews from Germany by Jews born in Israel.

Saint John of Acre – the port

The Crusaders occupied it in 1104, fortified it with **ramparts** and made it their capital city after the fall of Jerusalem. But today the only sign which remains of the now pitiful faith which inspired the Crusaders is an underground church with elegant ribbed vaulting in its crypt. An experienced eye can discern a fleur de lys carved in the stonework of the **crypt of Saint John**. Henri de Champagne had this flower engraved on his coins and it became the emblem of the French monarchy.

It was in Akko that Hercules was treated for a serious wound and according to certain authorities this was how the name of the city originated – in Greek *akko* means course of treatment or medicine.

Phoenician sailors used to burn saltpetre on the banks of 'the river of glass', the ancient Belus of the Romans. This was how the first glass utensil was born.

Until the development of Haifa, Saint John of Acre was the main port of Palestine. It is still the most important fishing port in Israel today. On the strand looking rather ridiculous, lies a rusty Turkish cannon which must have played some part in the defeat of Bonaparte in 1799. It was under these very walls at Akko, defended by Jezzar Pasha, that France ultimately and completely lost control of the route to the Indies. This Albanian adventurer well deserved his nickname of 'butcher' though his cruelty could not undermine his undoubted piety. In Islam and the East a warrior's prowess, even if it verges on bestiality, does not lack a religious dimension and resonance.

The mosque which Jezzar Pasha had erected in 1781 still bears his name. Its dazzling and triumphant whiteness radiates defiance skywards, particularly to all unbelievers. Its minaret has the air of a finger stretched out towards God, the beginning and the end of everything.

But, above all, Saint John of Acre is an extraordinary jumble of *khans* (caravanserai) which are the lifeblood of the ultra-oriental bazaar. It is in the shady nooks and crannies of the old Arab town, in the exotic souks, that you can enjoy to your heart's content the infinite mystery of the Orient with its traditional moneygrabbing and free-and-easy bargaining. Life is relished, unhurried and unsoured, in Saint John of Acre. It takes on a distinctive order where labour is a religious duty and not merely proof of a man's identity. Here laziness is an art whose cultivation demands many virtues.

You are constantly aware of the strong attraction this most sacred land had for the Christian soldiers who went on pilgrimages to Jerusalem, the stage of Christ's Passion; an attraction that has always nourished mass fervour. After Constantine the Great had constructed the Holy Sepulchre in Jerusalem and the Basilica of the Nativity in Bethlehem, the flood of pilgrims continued to grow.

Crusaders' ramparts

Saint John of Acre – the crypt of Saint John

Caesarea – the ramparts

Ruins of Belvoir

When the Arab conquerers invaded the Byzantine Empire the pilgrimages came to an end and were not resumed until the eighth and ninth centuries during the time of amicable relations between Charlemagne and Harun el Rashid of *Arabian Nights* fame. The protection of the Holy Places by the Franks was symbolised by the sending of the keys of the Holy Sepulchre back to Aix-la-Chapelle.

The Fatimid kings of Egypt who became the caliphs perpetrated the massacre of Jews and Christians and made Palestine run with blood. One of them, El Hakim, destroyed the Holy Sepulchre, and some years later after the Holy Places at Constantinople were also profaned in 1071, Pope Urban II decided to declare a Crusade at the Council of Clermont in 1095. Professional preachers whipped up religious fervour throughout Christian Europe. Wholesale slaughter ensued and the famous Jewish community at Worms was decimated despite the assurance of protection given them by the Bishop.

The First Crusade reached Constantinople about 1096. The soldiers were thus described by Foulques, the chronicler from Chartres, 'What an attractive and wonderful spectacle was presented by the brightly shining crosses of silk, gold thread and glowing red fabrics which the pilgrims had sewn on their papal insignia, on their cloaks and robes . . .'

When Godefroy de Bouillon took Jerusalem in 1099 Muslims and Jews were slaughtered. It was not until 1187 that Saladin cut the Crusader army to pieces at the Horns of Hittin in Galilee and the Crusaders were driven from the Holy Land. The Third Crusade led by Richard the Lionheart, Philippe Auguste and Frederick Barbarossa, never managed to reconquer Jerusalem. And so the Crusaders made Saint John of Acre their capital which it remained for the greater part of 100 years. The gothic architecture which they imprinted on the city still exists here and there . . .

The Crusaders, along with the Jews, were the only ones to have established an independent political entity in Palestine. The **ramparts at Caesarea** or Saint John of Acre bear historical witness to the faith that once foamed through Europe.

When you cross the fertile Plain of Sharon there, not far from Tel Aviv, is **Ramla**. Its tower is worth stopping and looking at. It dates from the fourteenth century and was originally the minaret of a mosque. Christians named it the Tower of the Forty Martyrs while to Muslims it was the Tower of the Forty Companions of the Prophet.

Ramla was the birthplace of Joseph of Arimathea who owned the tomb where Jesus was buried.

The tower at Ramla

2

Galilee and the North

'He who wishes to enrich himself should go up to Galilee.
He who wishes to become wiser should go up to Jerusalem'

The Talmud

Rosh Pina

In the wide and verdant region of Biet Hakerem (home of the vineyards), perched in the heart of **Galilee**, there is a small and almost unobtrusive little village called Peki'in. This little patch of ground has weathered all the storms which have racked and tortured Galilee and it has proved so desirable that the Jews named it 'the region of nations' (the Galil Hagoyim of which Isaiah spoke). With a tenacity born of faith an old Jewish family, the Zenatti, have clung to this man-made island of Peki'in. This family is still there today, a living testimony to a Jewish presence which the rise and fall of occupying powers has never succeeded in uprooting, as eternal as the rocks which dot the winding countryside of the Galilean mountains.

The Galil Hagoyim has today become known simply as Galilee. The land has been transformed under the hands of the pioneers who have reconstructed it. They have planted trees on the bare hillsides and drained the once unproductive ground surrounding the ancient Lake Huleh. They have built up villages on the slopes, the first of which was **Rosh Pina** (meaning touchstone). They have also placed kibbutzim and mochavim in areas once polluted with marshland. And all the while their only support came from the echoes of the Prophet's words 'And they shall build up the old wastes, they shall raise up the former desolations, and they shall repair the waste cities, the desolation of many generations'.

You should have the Bible in your hand to appreciate the intricacies of the Jewish, Arab and Druze villages, which are wedged between the narrow little valleys that characterise a Galilee steeped in both the past and the present.

Galilee countryside

Beit Shean – Roman amphitheatre

Arabs in Galilee

In the highest region of Galilee the archaeology of the Hatzor area does its utmost to re-evoke to the smallest detail the victory of Joshua over the Canaanites. From the shores of the Mediterranean to the Valley of the Jordan this pleasant land abounds with broken stones, tells (the ruins of buried cities), grottos, mosaics and coins. All are traces of ancient civilisations destroyed at the height of their splendour.

Excavations carried out in the **Beit Shean** region have revealed dozens of descending layers said to date from the pre-Biblical era.

At the city gates an almost entire **Roman amphitheatre** has been resurrected. It is now surrounded by a park.

But Galilee also exists in the present. The strong heart of Galilee beats to the rhythm of hard work in the avenues of fruit trees carpeting the Plain of Jezreel, in the fields of olive trees sprinkling the Biet Hakerem valley and on the tended grass of the kibbutzim. Work which demands that in order to fulfil their hopes men should force a living from the land which would die if they were to abandon it.

The Arab minority, concentrated

today in what they call 'the triangle' (meaning Galilee), have finally accepted that the laws of progress are irreversible.

The streams, the vines thickly hung with grapes and the trees along the road in Galilee, all seem to sing in the soporific heat of a sun that makes even the labourers bent over their pick-axes wax poetical. The singing is loudest at olive-harvesting time. It was from the olive that the oil was extracted long ago to anoint those chosen by God, and it was to this oil that Israel was compared in the sacred books.

Safad (Tsfat in Hebrew) is perched on the invigorating heights of Mount Canaan. It is one of the four sacred Jewish cities; the others are Jerusalem, Hebron and Tiberias.

In a picturesque disarray of tiered **little alleyways**, winding lanes and tumbledown attic roofs, all contributing to the town's bohemian character, the mediaeval **synagogues** recount the history of the intimate relationship with God that Safad has long enjoyed.

Safad did not get into the history books because of its role as a refuge for the fifteenth century Spanish Jews fleeing from Torquemada, but because it was the cradle of the Zohar and the Cabbala, the esoteric Jewish philosophy embracing the resources of logic. 'Respect the divinity of the Most High in all things for the kernel of his divinity is imprisoned within the rind of matter'. This saying of Rabbi Isaac Luria, known as Haari (the Lion), still echoes through the dim vaults of the recently restored synagogues.

In particular the philosophical doctrine known as Tsimsoum (contraction) has survived from this great master of the Cabbala. According to this doctrine, the Infinite of its own free will contracted itself to give birth to the finite. Today Haari lies with other Cabbalists on the slopes of Mount Canaan. Not far away lie entombed a number of worn and worm-eaten books of the Talmud. The people of Israel have given writings a tomb because words too have a soul.

People used to tell tales about this or that great Rabbi from Safad who was more familiar with the avenues of the Talmud than those of his own city.

But today the birthplace of the Cabbala is a town where you spend your summer holidays and also a kind of Galilean Montparnasse where young artists in search of inspiration come to pay court to the muse of painting in the artists' quarter (the old Arab quarter).

You don't pay a visit to Safad to see the artists though, but to see the synagogues and the yellowed leaves of their Talmuds. This the pilgrims know well; they come here every year for the festival of Lag Baomer and gather at Meiron a few kilometres from Safad at the tomb of Shimon bar Yochai, author of the Zohar, written here in a cave where he took refuge for 15 years.

This Zohar is rather like the land of truth for adherents of the Jewish faith. Only rabbis who have broken with the Cabbalist practices have ventured here. Few have returned.

One legend tells of four rabbis who took the risk of infiltrating the inner sanctum of the Cabbala. The first died there. The second killed himself. The third went mad. The fourth 'entered and left it in peace'. This was Rabbi Akiva, master among the masters, glory and splendour of Israel.

Safad – street scene

Synagogue in Safad, the cradle of the Cabbala

On the main Tiberias road, barely a dozen kilometres from Nazareth, there is a peaceful and casual little village stretching out in the shade of olive trees, fig trees and pomegranate trees. This is **Kafr Cana**. Two churches, one Catholic, the other Orthodox, have been built here where it is reputed that Jesus changed the water into wine (John II, 1–11) during the marriage at Cana. This miracle is commemorated in the Franciscan church.

Cafe in Kafr Cana

This fifteenth century Franciscan church was built on the foundations of an earlier church from which some fragments of mosaic have been preserved. According to a dedication written on it in Aramaic the founder was a certain man called Joseph.

As for the Orthodox church at Cana, this was built in 1556 on the site of an old mosque. The wine jars which you are told are the original ones of the miracle may be of doubtful authenticity, but it doesn't really matter: they are there for appearance to make the story live again.

Cana was the birthplace of Nathanael (John XXI, 2) who was led to Jesus by Philip and who, renamed Bartholomew, became one of the Apostles.

On his return from Judea Jesus stopped once again in Cana and healed the son of a certain nobleman who was dying at Capernaum (John IV, 43–53).

A little further east **Mount Tabor** dominates the Plain of Jezreel. Mount Tabor was a place of the highest strategic importance. It was here also that the Transfiguration of Christ took place. On this mountain which towers above the peaks of lower Galilee, Jesus's disciples saw their Master's face illumined by a sudden brightness. St Matthew tells us 'After six days Jesus taketh Peter, James and John his brother and led them up into an high mountain apart. And was transfigured before them: and his face did shine as the sun and his raiment was white as the light. And behold, there appeared unto them Moses and Elias talking with him.' During the sixth century three churches were built on the summit of Mount Tabor in memory of the three tabernacles that Peter proposed to set up there in honour of Moses, Jesus and Elias. In the twelfth century the Crusaders built a church there incorporating an underground apse of Byzantine origin. Today Mount Tabor is crowned by a modern **Franciscan basilica** which was erected in 1523 on top of the remains of the Crusader and Byzantine churches.

Eleven years earlier, in 1511, members of the Orthodox church had built the Church of Saint Elias there beside the grotto of Melchisedek.

At the foot of Mount Tabor there is a little Arab village named Dabburiya, recalling the memory of Deborah the prophetess and judge of Israel who stood up against the armies of Sisera and conquered the king of Hatzor.

Further on, at the foot of the cypress-covered hills and nestled in

Franciscan basilica on the summit of Mount Tabor

the hollow of the Jezreel valley, is **Nazareth**. Neglected for centuries, sacked by the Byzantines and then restored by the Crusaders, it is today the third greatest city (after Jerusalem and Bethlehem) for Christian pilgrims. This lowly, almost chaste, town is wreathed in a halo of solemnity and seems permeated with the breath of the Gospels. Here is the grotto of the Church of the Annunciation where the Angel Gabriel appeared to Mary, saying, 'Fear not Mary: for thou hast found favour with God. And behold thou shalt conceive in thy womb and

Dan – the Canaan altar

Nazareth

bring forth a son, and shalt call his name Jesus'.

The Convent of the Ladies of Nazareth, the Church of St. Joseph and Church of St. Gabriel all claim the honour of being the site of the home of Joseph the carpenter'.

It is as pilgrims that everyone comes to explore the town where Jesus lived as a child.

Dan is the outpost of the country at the northern edge of Israel. It is placed

at the foot of Tell el Cadi (Judge's hill). Close to the gushing springs in the centre of the *tell* is the site of the old **Canaanite altar** which was built as a sanctuary by the Danites for their preacher Jonathan whom they carried off from the house of Micah the Ephraimite.

The Jewish religion demands a strict adherence to simplicity in its funeral rites but, after Hellenism came to Judea, tombs took on a more sumptuous guise. Monuments were built at the graveside and a substantial amount of a man's wealth was buried with him. A number of these **Jewish tombs** were closed off with heavy stone doors.

Nazareth – Jewish tomb from the time of Christ

Tiberias looks a rather sad and sombre city in its greyish clothing of basaltic stone. Its grimy and defaced ramparts clash with the pleasant greenness of the surrounding Galilean countryside. It has been ravaged by the occupations of Crusaders and Turks, and buffeted by the all too frequent earthquakes. All that remains of the ancient city which was built by Herod to flatter his master Tiberius, are a few Roman columns, skeletal traces of stadia or amphitheatres spared by the whim of fate. Tiberias broods silently beside its lake and only deigns to smile when the first rays of the spring sunshine caress it. Then the terraced cafés beside the **Sea of Galilee**, Lake Tiberias, open their doors to a picturesque and varied procession of customers and Tiberias bathes its greying skin in the warmth of summer. The city becomes full of light and gaiety, transformed into a summer holiday resort, a water-skiing and canoeing centre.

One can unwind beside this lake, known variously as Gennesaret, or Kinneret, as well as Galilee and Tiberias. Today, fed by the River Jordan, it forms Israel's major reservoir and its waters flow through a huge concrete pipeline as far as the borders of the Negev in the south. The lake is not only useful to the land of Israel, in addition it offers the visitor a view of serene beauty with the gentle, little waves of its tranquil and limpid waters lazily lapping the shore. There is an infinite tenderness emanating from Kinneret. (In Hebrew the word means lyre.) It is also a **fisherman's** paradise, teeming with fish.

Jewish tradition (which has a legend for everything) explains in an unusual tale that one day the fish from the Dead Sea decided to settle themselves in the Sea of Galilee because they feared an apocalyptical end when Sodom and Gomorrah were destroyed.

It was from among the fishermen on this lake that Jesus chose his first disciples, Simon and Andrew, whom he changed into 'fishers of men'.

On the northern side of Lake Tiberias is the village of Capernaum, made famous by Jesus. It was here He preached the clearest of his sermons and where he healed the servant of the Centurion who, in gratitude, built the splendid synagogue which stands in the middle of the town.

A little further north is **Tabgha** where tradition places the miracle of the loaves and fishes. Mosaic tiled floors of Byzantine craftmanship must have paved an ancient church erected on the site of the miracle. Close to the river bank and commanding the ground above the lake is the **Mount of the Beatitudes** which Christian tradition reveres as the probable site of the Sermon on the Mount: 'Blessed are the poor in spirit: for theirs is the kingdom of heaven'.

To the east of the Mount of the Beatitudes is the

Sea of Galilee (*top*)   Tabgha – mosaic paving (*below*)

Ramparts of Tiberias (*top*)   Galilean fishermen (*below*)   Church of the Mount of the Beatitudes (*top*)   Sea of Galilee (*below*)

Hittin valley stretching out amid a scenery of winding rocks. The Crusader army suffered a bitter defeat here in 1187 from the forces of Saladin. It was here that the Holy Cross was lost and the gallant king Guy de Lusignan was taken prisoner.

Jethro, Moses' father-in-law, is buried here. That is why the Israeli Druze make an annual pilgrimage to the gorges of Hittin, to the tomb of the man from whom they claim direct descent.

The Bible itself calls Jethro the ancestor of the wandering Kenites, actually talking of nomads 'wandering in the Emek Jezreel'. Whatever you might think, specialist historians have agreed to acknowledge that the Druze living in Israel are the direct descendents of those Bedouins who appear in the sacred writings.

The great gathering of Israeli Druze takes place before the sanctuary of Kfar Hittin on 15th August, the supposed date of Jethro's (or Nebi Shaib's) birth.

You must not leave Tiberias and the surrounding area without an excursion to see the **hot springs** where old and infirm Romans used to come and bathe when the ancient city of Herod still existed. Tradition is long-lived in the Holy Land. From that time onwards the whole country spoke of the Hame Tiveria (hot springs of Tiberias). They often play a part in Israeli comic sketches too. But whatever they are, they have become the recommended and almost magical

The Hittin Valley

elixir to take for rheumatic aches and pains.

What was the origin of these healing waters and why should Tiberias possess such beneficial springs? Everyone has his own answer to that question. But the mystics and sages of Judaism are convinced that Tiberias owes its miraculous and lifegiving springs to the proximity of the sanctuary of the famous Cabbalist Rabbi Meir Baal Haness (Meir, master of the Miracle).

It is true that Rabbi Meir's life was an unbroken succession of miracles . . .

At the foot of the old town is a pantheon sacred to the famous doctors of the Jewish law – such as Rabbi Akiva and the great Maimonides. It is a testimony to the extraordinary intellectual influence that Tiberias experienced after the destruction of Jerusalem. Tiberias was where the Sanhedrin sat, the ancient judicial and legislative body that reigned supreme. Here too the Mishna and Gemara, which form the Talmud, were completed, written down and put in order.

Jewish volunteers from the Persian campaign (which ended with the fall of Jerusalem to the Byzantines) also came to Tiberias in 614 AD. It was the scene of the teachings of the ardent Rabbi Akiva prematurely left-wing defier of emperors, whom Jewish legend credits with having a lifespan as long as that of Moses and Hillel – 120 years. He was condemned to death because of his support for the heroic rebellion of Bar Kokhba. The Romans flayed him alive (the legend adds) on Yom Kippur, the Day of Atonement.

On the side of Mount Hermon to the north of Lake Tiberias one of the three affluents which unite to form the River Jordan, **the Banias**, bursts forth in a sparkle of snowy white water.

From the **grotto of Banias**, so called because it was thought of as a sanctuary for the local gods whom the Greeks classed together as Pan (because the letter 'p' does not exist in Arabic the resulting 'Panias' became Banias), the river gushes out in a torrent then suddenly becomes gentler before it pours elegantly into Lake Tiberias.

Herod's son, Philip the tetrarch, made Panias the capital of Galilee at the beginning of the Christian Era. He named it Caesarea Philippi to distinguish it from the Caesarea on the coast. And when the doctors of the law talk of Caesarea in the arguments in the Talmud, it is this little Caesarea Philippi to which they refer.

Banias is reputedly one of those towns visited by Jesus and his disciples. There have been several partial attempts at archaeological excavations in the area. **Sculpted niches** have been found in the rock face near the entrance to the grotto. There is every reason to suppose that the vestiges of the Roman times which are often visible above ground come from buildings constructed by Herod or Philip.

Before going on further you should take a last look at the western shore of Lake Tiberias, more especially at Beit Yerash. This grove of palm trees bears the name of Rachel, one of Israel's most sensitive poetesses. Although she died young Rachel Blaustein (1890–1931) nevertheless became in only a few years a symbol and a flag-bearer for her country. Her poetry quivers with joy like the trees of which she writes. The trees, the work, the love of the country, the beauty of its lake and 'what if all that had

Banias – sculptured niches in the rock face

never come into being?' she asked.

People know her poetry by heart. It has given gladness and hope to a whole generation of pioneers. Today the same songs are sung by Israeli schoolchildren:

My country, I have not sung your praises
Nor rendered your name glorious
By death-defying actions
Or by the plunder drawn from battle.
My hands have only planted a tree
On the tranquil banks of the Jordan river
My feet have only marked out a winding path
Through your fields.

Ein Machoresch kibbutz – the nursery

Tractors on a kibbutz

Karmiya kibbutz – mealtime

It was in 1909 that a handful of Palestinian Jews from Jaffa deliberately set out to build the most aggressively modern city back to back with their own. The result was the too-European Tel Aviv. In the same year the pioneers, dreaming nostalgically of a Tolstoyan world, founded Degania on the shores of Lake Tiberias. And so the first **kibbutz** was born.

Rid of the hedonistic temptations of city life, more or less freed from the influence of money, liberated from the hampering chains of the traditional Jewish family of the *shtetl*, the age-old ghetto, the kibbutzniks consciously fled from the feverish bustle of the metropolis to the bucolic pleasures of the country. They had to work physically at this return to the land in the manner propounded by A. D. Gordon, one of the craftsmen of this skilfully balanced mix of Zionism and socialism which formed the ideology behind the Degania kibbutz.

University graduates burned their degree certificates without many regrets and exchanged their pens for farm implements. Professors did not hesitate for long over leaving their chairs in order to learn to drive tractors. They had to change their whole lifestyle; a social revolution was in progress and the agriculture of the country needed more brawn than brains.

This revolution had a name of its own – the kibbutz. The kibbutznikim had been disillusioned by the Stalinist influence in the Bolshevik revolution in which some of them had taken part, and they wanted to show in a practical way that a marriage between socialism and liberty was possible. Stalinism had not utterly destroyed their faith.

What exactly is a kibbutz? It is a social microcosm, a

phalanstery where the socialism of tomorrow is practised with the emphasis on social justice. It is a small agricultural or industrial community where nothing belongs to any one person and where everything is under common ownership. Individualism has no place here and money is shunned, if not unheard of. Although 'discipline' is to be found in the kibbutz vocabulary, the word 'authority' does not exist. Everything reminiscent in even the slightest degree of the bourgeois world outside (even down to wearing collar and tie) is banned from the kibbutz. The most daring innovation, and the one open to the most criticism, is that of the bringing up and education of the kibbutz children, which is a communal affair. But does all this make the kibbutznikim communists? The pioneers there quote more readily from Isaiah than from Marx.

When all's said and done, the kibbutz belongs to that category of things which Shakespeare describes as being of 'such stuff as dreams are made on'. The kibbutz is a dream that has come true, something unreal. 'From another place perhaps' said the writer Amoz Oz who lives in the Hulda kibbutz near Rehovot. Everyone on the kibbutz is aware that this avant-garde figure has been widely acclaimed and his literature translated in some measure throughout the world. Yet everyday life has not changed for this writer, apart from the fact that the general assembly of the kibbutz has recognised his need for a typewriter and a room of his own for his nightly meditations.

Today there are 85,000 Israelis living in almost 250 kibbutzim. It is true that they represent only 4 per cent of the country's population but they contribute 12 per cent of the gross national product. And the kibbutz influence in every walk of Israeli life is undoubtedly much more important than the percentage it represents in terms of population. There is, for example, its considerable contribution to agriculture, well illustrated by the variety of cultivation stretching out in a fantasy of geometric shapes beneath **Tell Meggido** which overlooks the Jezreel valley.

Tell Meggido and the Jezreel Valley

Every kibbutz (formed from anything from 60 to 6,000 members) is more or less officially affiliated to one of the many parties on the chequered political scene. It is not only religious communities that have their own kibbutzim. Every kibbutz in the country does not share the same political, economic and social ideals. Conflicting ideologies at times create incompatible rivalries, though the National Federation of Kibbutzim to which they all belong ensures a peaceful co-existence.

Does this make the kibbutz a sterile society? On the contrary it changes from day to day. Its inhabitants are pragmatists and change direction every time they feel they are on the wrong track. Principles never take priority over people. If a principle does not achieve individual happiness and freedom then it is regarded as a bad one. That is why the kibbutz is forever reshaping its structures, reforming and trying to adapt itself to the multifarious demands of a permanently changing society.

On occasions the kibbutz has been converted to industry very rapidly, though not without protest. The laminate

Oren in Galilee. But enough said about their role as steward. This 'utopian kingdom' also offers spiritual adventure to those who seek it. Here young students in search of self-knowledge, refugees from middle-class life or merely curious tourists (when not spending the weekend **skiing on Mount Hermon**) come to take part in the **gathering of the cotton** which is one of the ceremonial occasions of the kibbutz.

A number of sociologists, not only from Israel, have recently taken a great interest in the kibbutz's state of health. Several of them have talked about crisis-ridden societies and small islands of socialism in a capitalist ocean. After extensive investigations, the sociologist Georges Friedmann is still a believer in the beautiful dreams of the kibbutz prophets.

Can it then be considered an anachronistic enterprise, or merely a staging-post in the agricultural colonisation of Israel? Or is it just a strange craze of youthful folly? To be truthful, the kibbutz is still searching for the right track while taking great care not to become a soulless society or

Skiers on Mount Hermon

Gathering the cotton

factory of the Afikim kibbutz which works in wood imported from Africa, is one of the best known in the country. Often the kibbutz appoints itself the administrator of luxury motels with swimming pools and bungalows aimed at the bourgeois city-dwellers who spend the weekends there. Two such are Ayelet Hashahar and Beit

betray the cause of liberty on the way. It is a unique and exemplary society discovering itself each day afresh and totally preoccupied with making the ideology serve the people and not vice versa.

The world has certainly not heard the last word from this, the city of the 'children of dreams'.

Mount Hermon (*top*)   A cotton field in Israel (*below*)

Despite its essentially changing character, the kibbutz remains, *nolens volens*, the finest (and only) blossom of the Zionist enterprise. It is also the touchstone of Israeli agriculture and the reservoir from which the country draws its men of valour and thinking statesmen.

At a time when the modern over-industrialised city of the Western world is becoming more and more of a concrete monster, full of fumes and noise, and when this urban environment has become hostile and oppressive, the kibbutz should continue its labours towards man's individual well-being in a climate of social justice, equality, liberty and a loving communion with nature.

Lower down the Jezreel Valley on the Huleh Plain the kibbutzim-tended fields provide a pleasant vista. You ought really to climb to the heights of Mount Hermon (2814 metres) to be able to appreciate the extent of the work involved. And you need to take part, if only once, in the kibbutz harvests which are celebrated with dancing and general euphoria, to fully understand that here work is more than a joy. It is a song, a redemption. The Jewish people who, long ago, were used to raising their eyes to the heavens in search of a Messiah who never came, suddenly discovered the harsher taste of the earth – and liked it.

In the shadow of the **Golan Heights, the Jordan** 'a yellow almost motionless river' flows so slowly and with waters so calm that Chateaubriand thought of them as 'thick'. The Jordan is indifferent to the change and the frantic pulsations emanating from the land which is constructed afresh every day. It flows slowly, almost with gravity, and ends up falling, exhausted by the length of its course, into the troubled waters of the Dead Sea.

Golan Heights (*right*)
The Jordan (*far right*)

3 & 4

Jerusalem

Jerusalem – the ramparts

'Ten parts of beauty were allotted the world at large: and of these Jerusalem assumed nine measures and the rest of the world but one . . .'

The Talmud,
treatise of Kiddouchine 49b

Jerusalem's name burns upon the lips of its lovers and it has unleashed men's passions for more than 40 centuries. Hearts have been broken here; vocations born. It is a city like no other city. No one can be a tourist here without being a pilgrim in the same breath, because you don't visit **Jerusalem**, you 'go up' to it. It is the crossroads of the great religions, the apotheosis and finality of every journey.

Everything conspires to make this city out of the ordinary. It has no river to water it, no valley opening out around it. Contracted, solitary, sometimes wild, always mystical, it is a place for adoration, contemplation and prayer, a city of religious fanaticism. Here the beggars are princes and the prophets have been inflamed with the fires of justice. Here is the fount of wisdom, 'For out of Zion shall go forth the law, and the word of the Lord from Jerusalem' said Isaiah the prophet of wrath.

Its history began with the dawn of mankind's history and now all the metaphors to evoke Jerusalem have been exhausted: throne of the Lord, navel of the earth, Queen of cities, capital of the universe. This city has suffered at the hands of the 'plunderers of the world' during 40 centuries of interminable occupation, in turn Babylonian, Greek, Roman, Byzantine, Persian, Muslim, Ottoman and British . . .

The old city and the El Aksa mosque

Jerusalem, the ecumenical city

Jerusalem, the capital of the Kingdom of David (1000 BC), sheltered the holy Ark of the Covenant, containing the tables of the law and the alliance. It is the city of Solomon's temple where the great Israeli prophets preached justice and equality. As well as being the scene of Christ's Crucifixion and the setting for his Via Dolorosa, it is a holy city for the Muslims, who venerate it as the spot where Mohammed 'rose into heaven' on his she-ass Bouraq. This ecumenical city is home to the three great monotheistic religions.

In the ancient kingdom of Israel the Jews were obliged to make pilgrimages to Jerusalem three times a year – at Passover, commemorating the leaving of Egypt, at Succoth, the reminder of the makeshift tabernacles which served the Jews during the Exodus in the desert, and at Shavuoth, commemorating the giving of the Ten Commandments on Mount Sinai.

The tradition remains today.

At the side of the road not far from the monastery of Latrun lie the skeletal remains of armoured cars, adorned with a few wreaths of faded flowers. Pieces of rubble from a former roadway dot the hillside. These pitiful remnants are left there to remind visitors to Jerusalem of the death of the Jewish soldiers who trod this **Road of Courage** in 1948 seeking to relieve the holy city.

A mile or so further on tapering columns of steel reach out and claw at concentration camps when Europe was insane and the world gone mad.

All at once the road which follows round the steep rocks capped by twisted pines, becomes an avenue. Hitchhikers, mainly soldiers, walk hopefully by the side. Then you reach the first-buildings hewn from the pink Jerusalem stone. A legal provision of the British mandate obliged the contractors to use only this Jerusalem stone for all the city building work. The stone itself plays a part in the mysterious aura of Jerusalem, giving an impression of the eternal, stemming from the marriage of the stonework and the light radiating from it.

It is flooding, dense, scouring, purifying light. It strips and dissects

At the roadside

the sky. This austere piece of sculpture is designed to remind those entering Jerusalem of the holocaust and the heroism of the Jewish people. Over the mountains of Judea, all around the Road of Courage and this memorial sculpture, 6,000,000 trees have been planted as a tribute to the 6,000,000 dead, slaughtered in the furnaces of people and things right down to their basic contours, baring the essential truth. The deeply serene blue of the sky combines with the brilliance of these ageless stones to bear witness to the timeless, uninterrupted presence of God. It is, or so the legend says, the breath of God that lightly shakes the leaves on the olive trees.

There is a little kingdom in the heart of the city indifferent to the hustle and bustle of modern-day Jerusalem. A happy community despite its cramped and shaky, harrassed and dilapidated, appearance, it is called **Mea Shearim** (the hundred doors). Unlike everywhere else in the country, the streets in this quarter are not named after Zionists leaders. Here they pay homage to the kings, prophets, sages and doctors of the law. Mea Shearim is a stronghold of orthodox Judaism, the kind of little township where pious old men, pale students and women from another century seem to be on intimate terms with the Ineffable. The inhabitants are known as the **hassidim** and are adepts at hassidism, the 'subversion through enjoyment' movement born in eastern Europe during the eighteenth century. You will be aware of them going about their work and their national duties. Vendors of *falafels* (a kind of spiced sandwich) or religious objects, publishers of holy books by scribes, rabbis or students, all gather in the evening, at the hour of the *maariv* prayers on the gloomy benches of the *yechivot* (Talmudic schools) for the *pilpoul* (philosophical debates) and study. Their goal is not apparent to us, but they don't care because they themselves know what it is – each evening they have an appointment with the Absolute.

At dusk on a Friday evening, or more exactly at 'Bein hachemachot' (between two suns) as they call it, there is an incomparable time when Jerusalem seems to stop breathing. The Mea Shearim district changes appearance. It is the Sabbath. The town and its inhabitants get ready to celebrate their daylong engagement with God. The hassidim, dressed in their white silk caftans and fox-fur caps (the *shtreimal*), make their way to the places of prayer, illumined by their inner dreams.

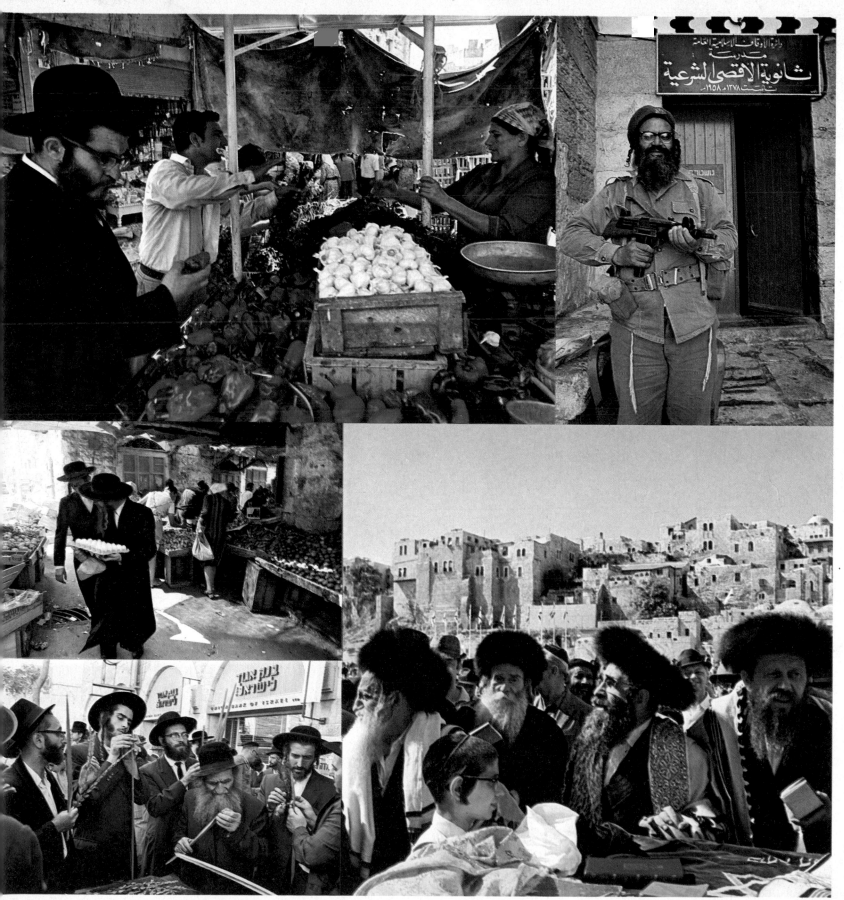

Jerusalem – Mea Shearim, the Hassidim district

Hassidim at the Wailing Wall. Behind them is the old city

Here, as you may already have guessed, is an enclave of eternity and more, of hope. And should you be walking along feeling sceptical or anxious, with eyes fixed on the ground, there will always be an old hassid around to break into your thoughts and exhort you to 'Look towards heaven. Man's eyes were made to contemplate the heights, it is a sin to look and feel sad'. Or else he will say

'The greatest sin is to give in to the spirit of temptation that convinces a man he is not a prince'.

Up until 1967 the inhabitants of Jewish Jerusalem would climb up the Tower of Ymca (a meeting-place for the young people) or to the summit of the Talpiot quarter (an old den of thieves now turned into an affluent residential district) so that they could gaze at the eastern part of the city.

Between the central thoroughfare (Rehov Yafo) with its European-type shops and the narrow streets of the old town was the Mendelbaum Gate. Here was the barrier which cut in two the city whose name means peace.

Since 10th June 1967 Jerusalem has once again been reunited. Those who saw the tears of the soldiers, and the children running along the road through the Hinnom valley, past

Jerusalem – The Western Wall, called the Wailing Wall

Young Hassidim

A Hassid during morning prayers

Mount Zion, to emerge at the Kotel Hamaaravi, **the Western Wall**, known as **the Wailing Wall**, know what depth of emotion was released when the people realised that Jerusalem would stay united.

This wall is something of a tribute to the past greatness and hours of glory of Israel. Today it forms the collective memorial of a whole race, being the only remaining trace of what was the Temple of Jerusalem. Ten centuries before the start of the Christian era, King Solomon built a sanctuary on Mount Moriah (where, according to tradition, the sacrifice of Isaac had taken place). This was to house the sacred Ark of the Covenant and was to become the shrine of priestly service and sacrifice. Today orthodox Jews still adhere in some small way to this tradition by sacrificing chickens on the eve of Yom Kippur.

In 587 BC King Nebuchadnezzar ordered the destruction of the city. In front of the ruins of the temple the fiery prophet Jeremiah bewailed 'How doth the city sit solitary, that once was full of people!'

And the voices of the exiles in Babylon came back to him like an echo, 'If I forget thee, O Jerusalem, may my right hand forget its cunning'.

The hassidim of **Mea Shearim** and orthodox and traditional Jews alike, throughout the whole of the world and under all circumstances, in happiness and sorrow, have re-echoed that phrase. It is a kind of talisman proclaiming the faithfulness of the people for a city they love passionately. This love is particularly apparent on the sorrowful day of Ticha Beav, when the Jews commemorate the destruction of the Temple.

Liveliness and fervour, ecstasy and faith, singing, dancing and prayer are the elements by which the hassidim of Jerusalem live, and die. God is not a stranger here. He is an ever-present companion, a friend who is both familiar and inaccessible. The lords of this city are poor men who have deliberately chosen to be so for the hassidim tradition acclaims and glorifies poverty.

Jerusalem – Mea Shearim district

The Mount of Olives – the tomb of Absalom (*above*) and the tomb of the Judges (*below*)

burn and loot, they razed it to the ground. Only the Western Wall remained and this was to become the heart and symbol of an exiled people buffetted throughout history by events over which they had no control. Throughout the centuries the stones of this wall have borne witness to the everlastingness of Israel; such stones have a soul of their own. Every generation of Jews for 19 centuries had these stones in mind as it thought 'Next year in Jerusalem'. After the 1967 war it was to the stones of this wall that thousands of Israelis and simple tourists entrusted their hopes and prayers, written on prosaic pieces of paper.

'There are men with hearts of stone' goes a popular Israeli song. 'There are also stones with hearts of men'.

As they face the wall throbbing chants, sighs, cries of joy or love, mysterious murmurings and whispers, the hassidim are permitted (or so the legend goes) to 'grasp the throne of the Divine with their human hands'.

And it is also overlooking this wall, on the Mount of Olives, which can be seen from the esplanade, that generations of Diaspora Jews have hoped to sleep their last. Some of them have even sworn it to their children.

At the foot of the Mount of Olives, not far from the new university, stands **the tomb of Absalom**. It is more than 20 metres high and cut from the rock in the shape of a Chinese hat. Nearby is the mausoleum of the Hezir family, the members of which were priests who served in the temple. It is generally agreed that this tomb is the sepulchre of James, the brother of Jesus and the first bishop of Jerusalem.

In *The War of the Jews* the historian Flavius Josephus evokes **the tombs of the Judges** of Israel in the valley of Kidron.

It is in this valley, declared the prophet Joel, that the trumpet for the Last Judgement will be sounded.

During the reign of Herod the Great, at the beginning of the Christian era, the second Temple was built. It was to be the most impressive sanctuary in the world, a temple in keeping with the grandeur of Jerusalem. The Talmud spoke of it in glowing terms, 'He who has not seen the building of Herod has never seen a beautiful building in his lifetime'.

But the **Temple of Herod** suffered the same fate as the Temple of Solomon – when Titus and his Roman legions set fire to it. 'I cry day and night over my temple' goes one of the many elegies chanted in the synagogue on the day of Ticha Beav. And the Romans were not merely content to

Stones from the temple of Herod

Every pilgrimage to Jerusalem is really a delving into the origins of faith. To Christians also the stones of this city tell a tale, each one seeming to mourn Christ's Passion; every alleyway along the Via Dolorosa murmurs an echo of his footsteps. And that flagstone, now worn down with the tread of men and beasts of burden, witnessed him stumbling by, laden with the weight of his cross.

The traditional Christian pilgrimage (following that of the Jews' 'going up' to Jerusalem for their important festivals) appears to have been inaugurated in the fourth century after the building of **the Church of the Holy Sepulchre** by Constantine the Great, who also built the Basilica of the Nativity in Bethlehem.

Constantine, a convert to Christianity, made it the official religion of the Roman Empire. One day he decided to replace the pagan temples with sanctuaries marking the life and death of Christ. The Holy Sepulchre was the most impressive. It was built on Mount Golgotha (the site of the Crucifixion), crowning a tomb which was known by its Greek name, Anastasis, or place of the Resurrection.

It was destroyed by the Persians in 614 then again in 1010 by the Caliph Hakim. The Crusaders rebuilt it with great ostentation in 1144.

The rock of Calvary was decked out in marble and around the sepulchre itself were placed a marble balustrade, a bell tower and several chapels including **the Greek Orthodox Chapel**.

Jerusalem – the Church of the Holy Sepulchre

Church of the Holy Sepulchre
Greek Orthodox Chapel

Even a guide has trouble in keeping his bearings in such a maze of chapels. An extraordinary diversity of cults is reflected in the liturgies, the costumes and the languages of the preachers. Among them are Ethiopian, Abyssinian, Russian, Greek, Armenian, Coptic, Syrian and Chaldean preachers. There are more Christian rites here in Jerusalem than in any other

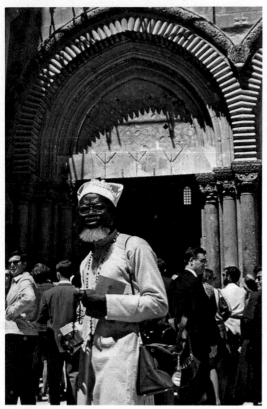

Ethiopian preacher in front of the Church of the Holy Sepulchre

At the entrance to the church there is an alcove padded with cushions and reserved for the Muslim porter, a member of the Jerusalem family Nousseibeh which has had the hereditary charge of keeping the keys for **the Holy Sepulchre** for centuries.

The restoration of the building after a fire in 1810 was by a Mytilene architect, Kalfa Kommenous. In the sepulchre itself a marble altar stone covers the actual tomb which is hewn out of the rock below and can only be reached by stooping, and then only by three or four people at a time.

Every Christian sect has a tiny chapel here among the pillars in the ambulatory. And it not surprising that every lamp, carpet and curtain here is a subject for dispute.

Church of the Holy Sepulchre – Abyssinian Chapel

place in the world. It was this fact that led André Chouraqui, the historian and deputy mayor of Jerusalem, to describe his city as 'the laboratory of true unity ... the pole, centre, the garden of a glorious humanity which seeks and finds itself and is reborn on the horizons of a new ecumenicalism'.

Dominus flevit

Here and there are dotted sanctuaries. They mark the Way of the Cross, that sorrowful route taken by Jesus from his entry into Jerusalem until his death on Calvary. Pilgrims, who come here in great numbers all year round, tread this path today; and also relive with Christ the journey leading to Bethany on the southern slope of the Mount of Olives. He stopped there as was his custom at the house of Mary, Martha and Lazarus. There, according to the Gospels, he raised Lazarus from the dead and today the greatest attraction of the Arab village El Azarieh (named from Lazarus) is a modern orthodox church of Muscovite design.

On the edge of the Kidron valley at the point where the Bethany road crosses the Jerusalem road, is a little Franciscan church built by the architect Barluzzi in 1955. It is renowned because it bears the name **Dominus flevit** (The Lord Wept) and the tradition goes that it was upon this spot that Jesus lamented the catastrophe which would overtake Jerusalem, saying 'If thou hadst known, even thou, at least in this thy day, the things which belong unto thy peace! but now they are hid from thine eyes. For the days shall come upon thee that thine enemies shall cast a trench about thee and compass thee round and keep thee in on every side. And shall lay thee even with the ground and thy children within thee; and they shall not leave in thee one stone upon another; because thou knewest not the time of thy visitation.'

On the Mount of Olives, where several roads meet, is **the Garden of Gethsemane**. This was an olive grove where Jesus and his disciples went to rest before continuing their journey. Saint Luke recalls that they spent the night there. In this garden 'He was withdrawn from them about a stone's cast, and kneeled down, and prayed'.

This was also the scene of Jesus's arrest and he was led under guard from the garden of Gethsemane to the house of Caiaphas, the High Priest. There Peter denied him. The house was on the side of Mount Zion and the spot upon which the Church of St. Peter is built is called Gallicantu (cockcrow), symbolising Peter's repentance. From Gallicantu Jesus was led away to the praetorium where Pontius Pilate awaited him. It is generally recognised that his trial took place at the Antonia fortress where Pilate lived. The Via Dolorosa begins at the foot of Antonia, at the spot where the Tower of David now stands. It was in the fourteenth century that the Franciscans started the holy office of the procession of the Stations of the Cross which still continues today.

After leaving the High Priest's house and before reaching the tower where Pilate was waiting, Christ and his escort had to climb the Lithostratus whose huge stones were deeply grooved to channel the rainwater into the cisterns.

The Church of the Garden of Gethsemane

Olive trees in the Garden of Gethsemane

The Via Dolorosa

Looking down from his judgment seat, Pilate dominated the scene. It was here that Jesus was flogged with the cat o' nine tails whose lashes were tipped with lead and bone.

Today **the Lithostratus** forms the cellar of the convent of the Sisters of Zion. On the flagstones you can still make out engravings from games of knuckle-bones and hopscotch and a 'B' for Basileus (king) as well as a crown of thorns. These stem from a pastime practised by the seasoned soldiers whose games were enlivened when the stake was a prisoner whom the victor could crown with the circlet of thorns. It was thus that Jesus was scornfully addressed: 'Hail, King of the Jews'.

When the prisoner was led before Pilate once more he showed him to the crowd with the words 'Ecce Homo' (Behold the Man). Judgment pronounced, Pilate washed his hands and **the Via Dolorosa** to Calvary commenced.

Most of the Stations of the Cross are marked nowadays with chapels. Each Friday, about 5 p.m., a procession of pilgrims treads the way of the 40 Stations. They climb the Via Dolorosa with the fervour and passionate emotion which characterise the oriental Christians. Ecclesiastical dignitaries follow the procession, filling the narrow souk-filled alleyways with their chants. Christians of all denominations take part.

In the Kidron valley is the sanctuary of **the tomb of the Virgin**, which owes its origin to the Queen Millicent who was the wife of Foulques d'Anjou and a great founder of monasteries.

But below, in front of the Western Wall, the Jews are already gathering to welcome the Sabbath while just above them in the courtyard of the Mosque of Omar, Muslims are kneeling and calling upon Allah.

In Jerusalem religion is only a question of which vows you have taken. Jews, Christians, Muslims, all experience the same glow and the same trembling in their hearts when they talk with God.

Their city is an embodiment of their religion. When he arrives in Jerusalem the pilgrim 'is filled with a deep and mystical joy. He enters an unknown world where joy is a thousand times more intimate, a thousand times deeper and more fruitful than in our world of pain'. (Dostoyevsky)

The Lithostratus

Jerusalem – the Temple esplanade

In their geography of sacred places the Muslims place Al Kuds, the holy city of Jerusalem, alongside Medina, the refuge of Mohammed, and Mecca, the capital of Islam. To them Jerusalem is the city of caliphs, Mohammed's disciples and the bearers of his message.

Mohammed, the founder of Islam and a courageous warrior, died in 632 upon which the spiritual and temporal reign of the caliphs began with Abu Bakr Omar. Six years after Mohammed's death Omar laid siege to Jerusalem and when the city surrendered Omar allowed the Jews to re-establish themselves in the sacred city.

On **the Temple esplanade** – which the Christians had turned into a rubbish tip – Omar built a wooden mosque. The octagonal mosque there today, which dominates the

Mosque of the Dome – the Rock of Abraham

old city (Haram-esh-Shait or Noble Sanctuary) still bears Omar's name though it was actually built by another caliph (Abd-el-Malik) several years later. In the centre of this mosque is **Abraham's rock** where, legend has it, the patriarch was prepared to offer up his son Isaac as a sacrifice. It was from this rock, too, that Mohammed ascended to heaven according to Islamic tradition. Mount Moriah, the Temple Mount, is the fountainhead for both faiths. Its stones symbolise the unshakeable unity of fervour in both Israel and Islam, as well as the insuperable dissension.

Once, under Muslim law, the Temple esplanade was forbidden to Jews. Today it is the rabbinical ruling that stops the Jews from using the esplanade. It is the most sacred place in Israel (even more so than the Western Wall), the Holy of Holies, and only the Chief Priest (Cohen Gadol) is allowed the privilege of going there on the Day of Atonement to pray, alone, for the safety of Israel.

At dawn on a Friday morning the voice of the muezzin from the mosque calls the faithful to prayer. The Muslims come flocking, take off their shoes, wash their feet and kneel to acclaim the glory of Allah and to ask for his mercy.

It was Suleiman the Magnificent who had the walls of the mosque covered in splendid Kashani tiles carrying inscriptions from the Koran. The arabesques – the only decorative motifs allowed under Islam – run the length of the wall of **the Dome of the Rock**. Inside the building contemplation and reflection are encouraged by an abstract symphony of marble, mosaics and precious carpets.

Not far away and lower down is the less prestigious El Aksa mosque, a stocky silvered building which was the work of Abd-el-Malik's son and built in the eighth century. Saladin presented this mosque with the mosaics on the dome as well as the *mihrab*, a kind of prayer niche reserved for the Imam. The reconstruction of the present mosque was completed in 1943. Eight years later King Abdullah, father of Hussein of Jordan, was shot dead here by an Arab nationalist. In 1969 a misguided young Australian, suffering from delusions of mysticism and mythomania, tried to set fire to it.

Jerusalem has undoubtedly attracted religious fanatics from the beginning. The prophet Isaiah declared, 'For Zion's sake will I not hold my peace'. The poet Yehuda Halevy, a Spanish Jew, was trampled to death by an Arab horseman while prostrating himself in front of the Wailing Wall. Halevy, better than anyone (in the fifth century), had immortalised Jerusalem.

'Your air is the life which the soul breathes,
Your grains of sand are grains of myrrh,
Your flowing waters streams of honey
In which I would walk naked and barefoot,
Amid the mourning and the ruins
Where the holy Temple stood,
Where the holy Ark was hidden,
Where the Cherubim concealed themselves,
In the depths of the Holy of Holies.'

The living heart and soul of Jerusalem is hidden in the souks, on the stairways that sometimes lead to nowhere. From the eight gates, hollowed out in the wall by Suleiman the Magnificent, the alleyways of covered souks descend unevenly, worn down by the steps of millions of pilgrims and tourists. The same smile and the greeting 'Marhabane' welcome you in the tiny street stalls and in the restaurants with their rough spicy odours. And if these children of Jerusalem should pester you to buy fabrics, fruit or simple

Stairway leading to the Dome of the Rock

Hebron glassworks

souvenirs, don't forget that they are, in some measure, selling you a little of their permanence and wisdom too!

What tourists admire most in **the old city** of Jerusalem are the decrepit little alleyways, the motley crowd and the clamorous street markets. The Arab geographer, El Moukkadassi (who came from the Holy City) wrote of tenth-century Jerusalem 'From the Holy City come cheeses, cotton goods, the famous grapes from Ainuni and Duri, delicious apples, bananas and a fruit which looks like a cucumber but whose skin peels off and whose flesh is not unlike that of a water melon – though more tasty and luscious, – pine cones as well as looking-glasses ... The best honey comes from Jerusalem where the bees gather nectar from the thyme.'

Jerusalem – street in the old city

Arabs in the old city

Jerusalem – tea merchant

The old city

Here you can sample the true spirit of the people in the whirlpool of acrid odours, colours and sounds. You can cast an indulgent eye on the teeming confusion of people and beasts of burden, ragged children, meat stalls frequently buzzing with flies, taverns serving exotic drinks. From the crowd rises a dull hum of conversation, interspersed with shouts and greetings of 'Salam' or 'Shalom'.

But wherever you find yourself in this city, whether in the Muslim, Jewish or **Christian quarter**, you will be aware of its picturesqueness stemming from its calm and unassuming people.

That tramp strolling around over there could be a prince and never know it, so lost is he in his dreams.

Christian quarter in the old city

And if a child in ragged clothing, but with the face of a prophet, accosts you on a street corner and demands some money to act as your hypothetical guide round his domain, then pay him with good grace for he is as beautiful as his city. Charity in Jerusalem is not, as it is elsewhere, the luxury of a good conscience. It is a heartfelt duty.

Lipchitz the sculptor
in the gardens of
the National Museum

The new Jerusalem has taken good care not to succumb to unbridled modernity or to poor quality in its building, as it has spread outside the walls of the old city. To the west in the peaceful middle-class quarters such as Rehavia the stocky massive houses are of the same pink stone as gives the rest of Jerusalem its timeless aspect.

As well as being the political, administrative, cultural and intellectual capital of the state of Israel, Jerusalem is also the religious capital of Judaism. The city has most willingly given up the right of economic and business seniority to Tel Aviv (which the 'old lion' David Ben Gurion dubbed 'the new Babylon').

History has never endowed Jerusalem with a vocation for the world of commerce. Here gather the political and intellectual élite of the country, students and graduates, elderly doctors and state officials who frequent the Viennese cafes in Ben Yehuda Street.

The new city walls have not yet suffered the assaults of advertisements or political graffiti. And if you see children daubing the walls it is only in the area belonging to the **National Museum's young people's section**. There pupils decorate the city's walls and pallisades under the direction of recognised artists.

Until recently Jewish art had been exclusively devoted to the embellishment of religious rites and the objects used in them. As far as anything else was concerned it was forbidden in the Decalogue – 'Thou shalt not make unto thee any graven image or any likeness of anything . . .' In the Dias-

Pupils of the National Museum's young people's section

pora the Jews did not build stone temples: they wanted rather to be builders in time.

When the Israelis returned to 'normality' the interdict of the Decalogue was no longer totally respected. **The sculptor Lipchitz** poses in the Billy Rose Sculpture Garden at the National Museum: creator and creation appear to be motionless blocks moulded out of the same bronze.

Jerusalem had need of a national museum worthy of the inheritance of 2,000 years' exile amongst foreign cultures; a museum which would

enshrine the past for the future. In its divers departments this museum gives an abridged version of history. Ancient and modern sculpture co-exist there: aggressive works by Picasso, Calder, Tinguely carry on a kind of dialogue with the forceful Rodin bronze. Art overflows with freedom and joy here and calls out to man. There is the final impression of a communion born of the conjunction of two timeless orders – the happiness of a fully mature art form and a countryside which has always been under the gaze of God himself. Did not Bezalel, the biblical ancestor of the Jewish artist, mean 'he who is in the shadow of God'?

Elegant and discreet in design, the Israeli National Museum fits harmoniously into the surrounding scenery of Jerusalem. It is also notable for having as its objective 'to embrace all the art of the world'. For the time being the collections of engravings and drawings by Israeli artists are more numerous than 'rare pieces' but, despite this, the Israelis see it as an oasis of art in the Near East and have every confidence in its future:

Hollowed out under the ground in this musuem is **the Shrine of the Book**. The dome which covers it is shaped like the lid of the earthenware jar in which the Dead Sea Scrolls were discovered. The shining brightness of the porcelain, whose whiteness is almost unbearable in the sunlight, contrasts strongly with the total blackness of the basalt wall which faces it, symbolic of the struggle of the Sons of Light and the Sons of Darkness in the Essene doctrine. In the centre of a raised platform beneath the dome **the Scroll of the Book of Isaiah** is displayed, protected under glass panels.

The discovery of these manuscripts was, to say the least, unusual, if not fantastic. In 1947 a young Bedouin herdsman looking for his stray goats went into a cave, in Khirbet, a mountainous and desolate area overlooking the Dead Sea. There he discovered earthenware jars which held seven manuscripts. The result of this find was a revolution in historical and theological thinking in the West.

The seven manuscripts had belonged to the pietist sect which used to live in these caves – the Essenes. They lived a chaste life, totally withdrawn from the world, guided by a doctrine founded on the expectation of an apocalyptic end to the world, when there would be a Manichean-like separation of the Sons of Light (the pure, i.e. themselves) and the Sons of Darkness (everyone else). The first manuscript contained seven leathern leaves from the Book of Isaiah. These are about 2,000 years old and so pre-date by 1,000 years the oldest of other known Hebrew manuscripts.

Beside the leaves of the Book of Isaiah were four other scrolls: 'The Manual of Discipline' which regulated in every detail the daily life of the Essene; 'the Hymns of Thankgiving' the author of which speaks to God in a very personal fashion; 'The Commandments of Habakkuk' a commentary on this prophet's writings, devoted to happenings during the Essene period; and finally a sort of Jewish military code of the times, 'The War of the Sons of Light against the Sons of Darkness'. Also on display in the shrine are vestiges of the revolt of Bar Kokhba, dug up at Masada, and the Babata archives found at Nahal Hever.

Shrine of the Book – students consulting the Scroll of Isaiah

Jerusalem – the Scroll of the Prophet Isaiah (*above*)
in the Shrine of the Book (*below*)

You should also see the young artists' pavilion where future painters and critics are nurtured.

The first experience that young men and girls have during their military service, which they do at the age of 18, is generally a sort of long route march across their country. (Military service lasts three years for men, 18 months for women.)

At Masada the young soldier, armed with a rifle and a Bible (in a symbolic unity), takes an oath that 'Never again will Masada fall . . .'. In Israel if you are a patriot there is no room for chauvinism, nor for militarism, in a country where chiefs of staff go back to their tractors at the age of 40 – when they aren't made ministers! Military parades are rare and when they do take place they are designed entirely to reassure a population who still carry psychological, and in some cases physical, scars of the traumatic holocaust. And today's children being told about Auschwitz and Birkenau often ask with a heartbreaking logic 'But what was the Tsahal (Israel's army) doing then?'

The grandfather of the nation, David Ben Gurion, wanted this army to be a 'popular army of fighting men and humanists', destined to ensure the survival of the people because it is made up of the people. It is a guerilla army, often without a uniform, but with great faith and efficiency, an army which respects human life and dislikes killing.

It is in the Bible that Israeli soldiers find their favourite image of themselves; warriors who wait for the time when 'the wolf also shall dwell with the lamb' and 'they shall beat their swords into ploughshares'.

Jerusalem – military march-past to commemorate the proclamation of independence

Young Israeli girl soldier

Archaeology is a veritable national passion in Israel. In the first days of spring a whole section of the population is transformed into an army of moles lovingly caressing each mote of earth. The heroes of this national craze are Yigal Yadin, the army chief of staff and Moshe Dayan. This enthusiasm for excavation has a symbolic value; signifying the deeply-rooted passion of a people for their old and new land. It is a question of bringing to light vestiges of the Hebrew civilisation. The Jew has for too long been subject to the forces of history, a tenant of other nations in the Exile: from now on he will cling to his own geography and his own land.

This land has been overrun by passing armies and the target of occupying powers, has been the object of dreams and desires, all because of its situation – at the crossroads of two worlds, the East and the West. Dating from the Roman Empire are, among other artefacts, **glass vases** from the Herodian period. The Israelis have also found official **stamps** belonging to the tenth Roman legion, named Fretensis, in Jerusalem and Ramat Rahel. These date from the third century, the Antonian period. When the Byzantine Empire succeeded the Roman (300–640), the resulting art lost the characteristic Roman restraint and aristocratic virility, as witness the Byzantine **vases**.

Archaeological discoveries allow us to relive other times and an **ivory fan holder**, found in Akhsiv in the north of the country, 'speaks' to us of the Phoenicians (999–960 BC) and of the refined nature of their art which has proved a permanent challenge to Hebrew monotheism. This fan holder carries the name Abdubaal, evoking Baal, that Phoenician idol against whom the Jewish prophets never ceased to rail . . .

Idol-worship was ever present in this land which was always torn between the two temptations: that of a uniquely simple and austere faith with the inner grandeur of worshipping the One God, and that of the pomp and the orgies which characterise idolatry. At Avdat a **bronze panther** was found, sacred to Dionysos, the Greek god of wine, or perhaps to some oriental divinity. This reveals the spirit of first century art to us in the present day.

But above all the soil of this land tells us about the history of mankind. It is not by chance that the sages of the Talmud say that the first man was born here. In Lebeidya, south of Tiberias, the remains of the oldest man known in Israel have been found – fragments from the skull of Pithecanthropus. Art was already of an elaborate nature during the copper age (4000 or 3000 BC) when small urban communities began to evolve. A certain artistic refinement is discernible in their stylised figurines, such as the **standard-bearer's circlet** dug up near the Dead Sea.

Glass vases from the Herodian period

Byzantine period vases

Roman official stamps

Bronze panther of the first century

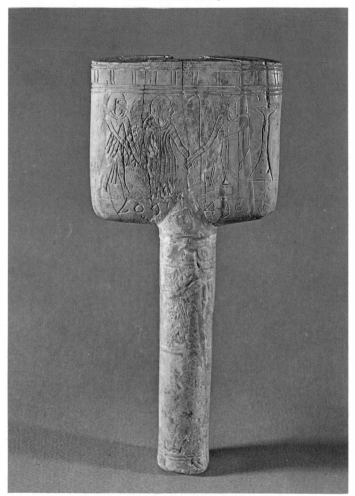
Ivory fan-holder from the Phoenician period

Standard-bearer's circlet (4000 or 3000 BC)

Only the Jewish people have prayed for this implacable country. During the Exile they prayed that it would rain and that the harvest would be abundant, even though they would never gather the fruits. Throughout 2,000 years only the Jew has turned in prayer towards Jerusalem, three times each day, for here was the only soil he had ever owned.

The hymn *Next Year in Jerusalem* sung by every exiled community is weighted with nostalgia and a fond hope. It became the Jewish slogan,

Jerusalem – the Knesset: entrance by sculptor David Palombo

their cry of anguish, their shibboleth. At the first Zionist Conference in 1897 at Basle Theodor Herzl, a Viennese journalist, disgusted by the Dreyfus affair, declared 'If you really wanted it, it would not merely be a dream!'.

Today the 500 deputies of Israel's parliament, **the Knesset**, sit under Herzl's portrait in an impressive building where there are works by Chagall and **a wall by Karavan**.

Israel is not only the state of the Jews. It means to be a Jewish state. Although there may not be any obligation on its citizens to be practising

Jews, they are nevertheless compelled to participate in a certain number of religious manifestations – they have, for example, to be married by the rabbis. This raises the problem of separating the synagogue and the state, something many deputies hope to achieve. Opinion polls taken in the country have shown however that the majority of the population would be against such a separation, were it to be adopted. They see it as a danger to Jewish unity. That is why, despite the criticisms sometimes levelled at the country's rabbinate, **Hechal Shlomo**, the seat of the two spiritual leaders of Israel (one Ashkenazi, the other Sephardi), has never been defaced by irreverent graffiti. The people are fully aware of the part that religion has played in the Israeli conscience; it has moulded the unique Jewish sensibility. It is a religion which, when all is said and done, has supported the hope of a people in waiting for 2,000 years on the paths of the Exile.

Chamber of the Knesset – the Dani Karavan wall

Hechal Shlomo, seat of the country's rabbinate

5

Judea and Samaria

The Springs of Elisha near Jerusalem

'Ye shall once again plant vines on the hillsides of Samaria.'

Jeremiah 31

'Get thee up unto Mount Nebo, which is in the land of Moab, that is over against **Jericho**; and behold the land of Canaan, which I give unto the children of Israel for a possession.' This was what God told Moses as he forbade him to enter the Promised Land. The Jericho of the Bible is situated further north than its present-day location, near the spring which feeds **the pools of Elisha**.

If we wish to decipher the message of this land of Judea we must imagine ourselves as Moses, on the threshold of death and eternity, gazing from afar at this land of which he knew nothing. Judea was the stage for the biblical drama of the greatest of the prophets, he who was the incarnation of the Promise made to the children of Israel.

To capture the beauty of an oriental dawn you need to climb the slopes of **Mount Scopus** very early in the morning, about four o'clock. A milky pallor gradually weaves a network of first white, then pink, threads across the dark sky. The sun stretches out its first rays which crown the summits of the Judean hills, changing from pink, through ochre to dazzling brightness. Purplish-blue gashes rend the sky. Then the golden mass of the sun lights up the summits with the blaze of a thousand fires.

The bare hills with their seemingly incandescent dust haze, the bluish shimmer of the distant Dead Sea, the sun playing on the sandy belt of desert, all make up a truly memorable sight.

Judea and Samaria have always been the gateway for invaders of the Holy Land. Today the land has painfully shaken off the phantoms of war. The different people merge: sunburnt Palestinian fellahs attempt to lead their daily lives in peace with the pioneers of Hebron who once more work the soil.

Enemies of yesterday now share the same activities, lavishing the same care on their crops. Today they are companions in the same destiny, tomorrow perhaps they will be brothers in the peace promised by the prophet Isaiah, 'Peace to him that is far off, and to him that is near'.

The oasis of Jericho. In the background is the city

Mount Scopus – view across the dip of the Dead Sea

91

Bethlehem – Grotto of the Nativity

Behind the densely populated suburbs of Jerusalem the road plunges deeply into the rocky Judean desert. Not far from Bethany, at the gates of **Bethlehem**, is the shepherds' field. There is a chapel over the cave where

Basilica of the Nativity
St. Helena's Chapel

Basilica of the Nativity
The Church of St. Catherine

Greek Orthodox service

they were resting before they were told of the birth of Jesus.

The name of this town, Bethlehem, means 'house of bread'. Christians have spoken it softly and with reverence throughout the centuries. Unassuming and contemplative, Bethlehem celebrates the Good News lost in prayer.

Jesus was born here. The pilgrim feels emotion rise as he approaches the silver star placed on the floor of the **Grotto of the Nativity**. On it one may read the Latin inscription '*Hic de Virgine Maria, Jesus Christus natus est*' (Here Jesus Christ was born of the Virgin Mary.)

This grotto arouses strong religious fervour and attracts countless pilgrims. But it was not without sadness that St. Jerome declared that 'The most sacred spot on earth is half-hidden in a copse dedicated to Adonis and in the cave where the Baby Jesus was born they used to mourn the death of Venus's lover'. The Empress Helena, mother of Constantine, had the first church built here in 325. She devoted her life to piety and to the veneration of the Holy Places and, naturally enough, **St. Helena's chapel** is dedicated to her.

At the far end of the grotto a door leads to the oratory where St. Jerome wrote the Vulgate, the Latin version of the Bible. From there you may pass through a tunnel into the **Church of St. Catherine** where the traditional midnight mass is held at Christmas.

Half-buried remains can still be seen today in the ancient Church of the Nativity. In 560 the Emperor Justinian had a basilica built on the foundations of Constantine's church. In the portal the Crusaders cut a pointed arch low enough to prevent the Saracens from entering on their horses.

The Basilica of the Nativity is the only building in the Holy Land in the pure Roman style. The Crusaders never stopped adding to it but the sumptuous mosaics which once adorned the Tree of Jesse have almost completely vanished. The Byzantine columns are still painted with the figures of western saints; Saint Leonard and Saint Cataldus of Ireland, Saint Margaret and Saint Bartholomew of Canterbury, Saint Canute of Denmark and Saint Olaf of Norway . . .

But the simple crosses cut by unknown hands into the stonework of the Grotto of the Nativity are even more potent signs of the tidal wave of faith which swept over the walls of Bethlehem.

Members of the Orthodox, Armenian, Catholic, Coptic and Abyssinian churches mingle here and add to the general fervour.

Oriental piety is often demonstrative: the holy merges into the picturesque. Processions which have retained their former ostentation and pomp are at the same time displays, pilgrimages and public affirmations of faith. The studied deliberation of learned prelates, the gravity of the faces filled with devotion, the slow progression of the men of God across **the main square of Bethlehem**, all are the perfect response to the enthusiastic piety of the masses.

On Christmas Eve the normally peaceful rhythm of life in Bethlehem quickens its pace. The town is gripped by a kind of controlled frenzy. The faithful, rapt in contemplation, curious and intrigued Jews, hippies lost in their private reflections, all join the procession, while bells and hymns announce the glad tidings.

But Bethlehem is not only the town where Christians come to drink at the source of their faith. It figures too in the most sensitive depths of the collective Jewish consciousness. For the faithful Jew, Bethlehem is the burial place of 'Our Mother Rachel'; Rachel who wept for her son's misfortunes (so the prophet tells us); Rachel who has become the model for and the blessing of Jewish motherhood. Her tomb attracts not only Jews but also many Muslims.

Religious procession

Countryside between Jerusalem and Jericho

same reverence and prayer. Here, according to the Pentateuch, Abraham bought the cave of Machpelah from Ephron the Hittite as a tomb for Sarah. Tradition has it that Abraham himself is buried here.

It was in front of Jericho that Joshua, Moses' successor and bearer of his message, incited the tribes to attack Canaan. The tribes of Judah, Benjamin and Ephraim shared the land of Judea and Samaria. At Hebron David was anointed king: on the death of Solomon, his son, the kingdom was split into the two rival states of Israel and Judah. Both were then invaded and their time of glory was past.

The Judea-Samaria guarded so jealously by Israel today also includes the colonies of Gush Etzion whose kibbutzim were wiped out during the war for Israeli independence in 1948. Nowadays the children of those who died there have come back and, imperceptibly, the confrontation of 'fire and blood' (which has always existed in this country where the two opposing races spring from the same father) is giving way to interaction and communication.

In Samaria in olden times Herod had built a Graeco-Roman copy of a forum, acropolis and palace. Some of the stone blocks came straight from the palace of Jezebel, the idolatress of Baal. Princess Salome's dance no longer echoes round the palace of Herod and the blood of John the Baptist has been washed away by the centuries.

The ancient dramas of the Orient have been succeeded by modern conflicts, though these are whipped up by the same myths and beliefs. Who can say what this Arab peasant is dreaming of as he sits in front of **the mosque at Sebast**?

Jericho, Hebron, Bethlehem and Shechem (Nablus) have a familiar ring to the ears of an Israeli child, or any Jewish child for that matter. They appear on almost every page of the Bible and the memories evoked by them went with the Jewish people into their long Exile.

The Israelis rediscovered these biblical sites in 1967, as though it was the most natural thing in the world, renewing an unbroken contact with their history and their ancestors.

Judea and Samaria were the setting for the patriarchs' extraordinary spiritual adventure. At Hebron God drew up the alliance with Abraham that was to make him the father-figure of two great monotheistic peoples, both descended from his line – Israel and Ishmael.

At the tomb of the Patriarchs in Hebron the two branches of Abraham's line meet and mingle in the

Remains of the old palace of Herodium

A potentate of foreign extraction, put on the throne by Roman imperialism, which made him the last Jewish Hasmonean king, a rigid ruler with a total devotion to Rome, an inordinate sycophant; this was Herod the Great.

His total submission to the cultural canons of the Roman Empire made him an advocate of Rome and Hellenism. Hated by the Jewish elite, he attempted to ingratiate himself with the common people by embellishing the Temple in Jerusalem and the tomb of the Patriarchs in Hebron.

But his personal inclinations led him rather to build impressive palaces and monuments of Graeco-Roman inspiration. Such was the **Herodium** near Bethlehem, a summer residence, built on a hilltop. You can still see today the outline of the four towers in the surrounding wall.

The building of such strongholds was specifically designed to keep the Jewish population (always ready to revolt) under surveillance.

Ridiculous Herod, whose palaces lie open to the elements: yet a simple temple wall which he had built by the poor people of Jerusalem has come to crystallise the tears and hopes of the Jewish people. Does not the Talmud say that virtue can come out of sin?

Aerial view of the fortress of Herodium

The Dead Sea – the name well becomes this pool of nothingness. 49 miles long and 11 across, 400 metres at its deepest, it is the lowest point in the world, 394 metres below sea level.

But these figures convey nothing of the poetry of its lunar-like desolation. The surrounding countryside and the lifeless greenish surface of the water, devoid of reflections, seem impregnated with a tragic solitude. The impression of anguish is suffocating; it fixes the eye so that it is gripped by the demonic grandeur of this lifeless sea.

Here the surface of the heavy brackish water is almost crushed by the weight of the sky. It is wild scenery, a fitting stage for the biblical drama of fire and suffering. The Dead Sea covers the ancient sites of Sodom and Gomorrah, those cities of total sin, full of injustice, where the poor, the orphaned, the stranger were all objects of hate. What could Father Abraham achieve in his pathetic pleading with God when there was not even one just man in Sodom and Gomorrah? Perhaps the fate of these impious cities is inscribed in the charred and cursed rubble scattered in this desert of death and oblivion.

The Dead Sea is certainly a unique spot in the world, where men can touch their own fragility. The surrounding country is made up of stalagmites of salt, snowy flakes and dried and petrified wood which writhe into this sea, called in Hebrew Yam Hamelah (sea of salt).

The salinity of the water is much too high to allow even the tiniest speck of life, so that there are no fish and no plant life. And bathing lasts only so long as the time needed for the taking of the traditional photograph of a man floating while reading his newspaper.

The Dead Sea – stalagmites of salt (*top*) and snowy flakes (*bottom*)

The Dead Sea

The Muslim sanctuary of Nebi Musa

On the road leading to Jericho, nestled among the barren hills, is **the Muslim sanctuary of Nebi Musa** (Moses the prophet) surrounded by the innumerable graves of simple believers.

Moses, chief among the religious founders, legislators and moralists, died on Mount Nebo on the seventh day of the twelfth month. No-one, the Bible tells us, has ever known the whereabouts of his grave. The greatest of the prophets and the humblest of men had lived in too close an intimacy with God ever to belong to the earth again. But the Sultan Saladin, so the story goes, had a vision in which he saw Allah move the body of Moses to this spot which is now the destination of a pilgrimage each Good Friday.

It was, in fact, more a question of politics than religion that influenced this sudden instituting of a pilgrimage to this sanctuary, which was built over a symbolic tomb by Sultan Baibars in 1269. The increasing number of Christian pilgrims to Jerusalem during Holy Week was undermining the Muslims' dominance over the holy city. And so, in obedience to the new custom, Muslims from all corners of Palestine gathered for prayers at Haram-esh-Sharif then made their way in procession to Nebi Musa and thence back to Jerusalem. This pilgrimage lasted precisely as long as Holy Week and was intended to stifle any inclinations towards a Christian revolt.

The splashing of its fountains and the accompanying shade of its gardens make Jericho an oasis in the desert. A **neolithic tower** (7,000 years before Christ), which was discovered at **tell es-Sultan**, proves that the city is one of the most ancient in the world.

During the conquest of Canaan, Joshua's armies, the Bible tells us, marched seven times around the city walls 'and on the seventh day the city fell'. The Book of Kings recounts how 'the men of the city said unto Elisha, Behold, I pray thee, the situation of this city is pleasant, as my lord seeth: but the water is naught, and the ground barren. And he said, Bring me a new cruse and put salt therein. And they brought it to him. And he went forth unto the spring of the waters, and cast the salt in there, and said, Thus saith the Lord, I have healed these waters: there shall not be from thence any more death or barren land. So the waters were healed unto this day, according to the saying of Elisha which he spake'.

Excavations carried out at Khirbet Mefjer have revealed the splendour of the ancient Omayyad palaces of the caliphs of Damascus. Khirbet Mefjer was the summer residence of Walid I. Its luxury was dazzling and some of its erotic frescoes recall the inferno of those at Pompeii. A life of indulgence is extolled in the fountains and colonnades, the baths and shady patios, the mosaics and arabesques.

Jericho – neolithic tower at tell es-Sultan

inspiration of his own, murmurs the words of love immortalised by Solomon in the Song of Songs to his girl friend. This pastoral poem, this unforgettable love song, today forms part of the Holy Books of Israel. Rabbi Akiva, the greatest of the sages of the Talmud, thought of it as 'the holiest among the holy writings of the Bible'.

For centuries different schools have differed over the correct interpretation of the Song of Songs. Some wish it to be seen only as an original and wonderful poem of love. But that is not the prevailing opinion: the majority of the great commentators see it as a symbolic poem, an allegory of the mystic marriage between God and the Israeli Knesset (the community of Israel).

But such theological disputes seem irrelevant among the welcoming and peaceful caves and springs of Ein Gedi. Let us not pursue further the meaning of this epic love poem; let us content ourselves with thinking that it contains the highest examples of the art of litotes.

Ein Gedi oasis

In the first chapter of the Song of Songs we read 'My beloved is unto me as a cluster of camphire in the vineyards of Ein gedi'. In the wilderness of Judea between the barren Dead Sea and the tragic buttresses of Masada, **Ein Gedi** (the Spring of the Kid) is an oasis, made for rest and enjoyment.

David took refuge in one of **the caves of Ein Gedi** when he fled from the wrath of Saul. But this haven of pastoral coolness with its propitious cave is best known as the setting for the turbulent love affair between King Solomon and the Shulamite woman. Fired by the feelings aroused by the eventful history of this poet-king, more than one Israeli youth, lacking

The springs at Ein Gedi

The caves of Ein Gedi

It is at **Masada** that the young recruits in the Tsahal (Israel's army) take the oath 'Masada will not fall a second time'. For it was here the 19 centuries-long Exile began.

The precipitous peak of Masada rises tragically and impressively. It is the most revered place of pilgrimage for the young generation of Israeli sabrim. The collective suicide of 960 zealots, besieged in the fortress by Roman troops led by Flavius Silva, fires the imagination of the young Israelis in a language they understand – the language of courage. For them Masada epitomises the freedom of a proud people, not the pawns of other races' whims (as they regard their fathers).

The precursor of this national cult of Masada is Yigal Yadin, archaeologist and chief of staff of the Israeli army. In 1963 he launched a worldwide appeal for volunteers and the work of the different teams led to the discovery of the treasures of this stronghold which Herod the Great made impregnable.

Gigantic cisterns, storehouses, synagogues, ritual baths, catapult stones, jewellery, bones, remains of provisions were all unearthed and brought out into the light of day. They tell the extraordinary story of these zealots who preferred death to dishonour.

Masada held out against the Roman invaders until 73 when Flavius Silva laid a long siege to it. Having built an access rampart the Romans then bombarded the Jewish fortress with huge stones, which still strew the ground today. Eliezar Ben Yair, the chief zealot, convinced his companions they should choose suicide.

The Jewish historian Flavius Josephus, chronicler of *The War of the Jews*, describes the scene which met the Romans once they had gained the summit of the fortress: 'They found a great number of dead. Instead of rejoicing at the fall of their enemies, the Romans could not help marvelling that so many Jews had made and carried out the same resolution, showing such contempt for death.'

Today the Jewish schoolchildren who visit this high point of Israeli courage know by heart the appeal of Eliezar Ben Yair to his companions at arms: 'For a long time, my brave companions, you have been resolved never to be servants to the Romans, nor to any other than to God himself . . . Let our wives die before they are ravished and our children before they taste the yoke of slavery . . . Let us spare only our provisions to provide tangible proof that we were not worn down by privation but, faithful to our first resolution, preferred death to servitude.'

The rock of Masada

Masada – giant cistern hollowed from the rock

The fortress of Masada and, below on the right, remains of the defences built by the besiegers

6

The Negev and the Red Sea

'The wilderness and the solitary place shall be glad for them: and the desert shall rejoice, and blossom as the rose.'

Isaiah

Hotel in the Negev

You must set out for **Beersheba** very early in the day when the torrid heat of the Negev has not yet quite stifled this lifeless plain and when the arid and deserted land is still covered in morning mist. Soon the burning sun will beat down mercilessly, crushing this barren waste which extends from Beersheba and Arad as far as the Gulf of Eilat. It is a vast triangular desert region, more dead than alive, and years of artificial respiration have scarcely brought it back to life.

The blocks of white concrete which herald the impressive capital of the Negev have an air of strangeness, almost unreality, standing as they do in the midst of the desert. Beersheba, a modern, bustling city lies at the very heart of this unproductive desertland. Its construction was a rushed job, without much architectural planning, because of the impatience of the immigrants wishing to settle here.

Beersheba in its role as the gateway to the desert is first and foremost a Bedouin city. The Bedouin with their wrinkled faces peering from beneath their traditional headgear, the *keffia* (a kind of white cloth with black fringes), are a familiar sight, strolling along and driving their camels in front of them with characteristic nonchalance.

There are about 30,000 who have chosen the nomadic way of life, risking the sun-baked tracks and pitching their tents along the way. At the end of the week they gather at the city gates for **the weekly market**. Sometimes the wind puts an end to this market and they go back to their camps in the brutal, savage desert which to them is a friend. They accompany the familiar murmurings of the desert wind with tunes played on instruments they fashion themselves.

　　　　　　　　　　　　　　　　Market day in Beersheba

The Bedouins are perhaps the last truly free men in the region, but will they soon be tempted into the comforts of urban civilisation? It appears that the building of a residential district near Beersheba has been foreseen for them at some stage in the future. Will they then agree to exchange their tents for concrete houses, their camels for cars, their keffia for lounge suits?

4,500 of them are today employed as agricultural workers in Israel and about 1,000 of them are members of the Histadrut. But even though they allow themselves to be tossed gently on the ripples of social change (such as running water and electricity), the Bedouin remain firmly attached to their individual idea of happiness. These sons of the wind and sun remain the faithful lovers of a desert which each day they learn to understand more fully.

Bedouin in their tents

The centre of Beersheba is a beehive of industry; wide avenues carrying streams of traffic, huge houses for American millionaires, discotheques; nothing is lacking here. But a cursory glance from one of the outlying buildings at the encroaching sand attacking the facade is all that is needed to understand that even the tiniest bit of life here represents a true victory against nature.

Twenty centuries ago, the Nabataeans also tried to push back the edge of the desert. These nomads, who were descendents of Nabath of Nabajoth, the son of Ishmael (himself the son of Abraham and Hagar) came from Arabia and settled in the Negev. They built towns, Avdat (today nothing more than a staging-post on the Beersheba-Eilat road) being one. They made the desert fruitful by catching and storing rainwater from the hills. And it was thus without the smallest oasis or spring that the Nabataeans made Avdat a watering-place, and the axis of the Negev between the Red Sea, the Dead Sea and the Mediterranean.

In Beersheba today the engineers at **the Arid Zone Research Centre** take a lively interest in ancient Nabataean history. Among the solutions they have come up with to overcome the water shortage problem are the desalination of sea-water, invented by the engineer Alexander Zarkhin, the exploitation of solar energy, and the age-old method of conserving the rare falls of rain. What is more, a national irrigation campaign is being studied which envisages using water drawn from Lake Tiberias to irrigate the whole of the desert by means of gigantic pipelines.

The Arid Zone Research Centre – solar oven

This constant struggle for water is the greatest problem in the region and it caused the cruellest hardship to the first pioneers here. The battle for victory in the Negev in 1948 is surrealistically portrayed in **the Palmach Brigade Memorial**, a huge sculpture by Dani Karavan, which stands on one of the Beersheba hills. Ben Gurion later said that this stretch of sand-dunes was dearer to his heart than the old city of Jerusalem. In the centre of the memorial a dome, split in two, like a broken heart, and riddled with holes, recalls the burst of shellfire. 'It evokes the memory of the dead at the same time as the fight for life' is how Karavan himself described it.

The scenery of the Negev looks apocalyptical but for men like David Ben Gurion it is also evocative of the beginning of a new world.

Ein Hatseva – peasant soldiers

Water, new roads, electricity and industry have all transformed the traditionally desert country of the Negev. The agricultural development of the desert has made the greatest impression in the Arava plain in the south. Thousands of hectares have been cultivated, fields ploughed, citrus groves planted. Agricultural villages have been founded and kibbutzim born in the land stretching from the Dead Sea to Eilat – **Ein Hatseva**, Ein Gedi, Ein Rakov, **Yotvata**, Grofit. The inhabitants share the same fixed objective, to make life spring from a mineral-impregnated countryside and make the wasteland blossom like the rose.

Not all plants can be grown in the Negev, of course, but some of them thrive better here than anywhere. The sultry climate of Arava is particularly suited for fruits and vegetables which are harvested four times a year, allowing tomatoes and new potatoes to be exported and sold at very competitive prices on the European market.

Fields of roses and gladioli are grown on the Yotvata kibbutz. Then, further south, at Be'er Ora, 'the well of light' (but called 'the well of shade and death' by the Bedouins), members of the Nahal, soldiers who work the land, have wrought real miracles in the agricultural field. In this rocky and swampy ground the pioneers have succeeded in artificially cultivating tomatoes, lettuces and haricot beans, all grown in simple tanks containing the appropriate chemicals.

In the Negev more than anywhere else the young people have turned imagination into action. There is really something miraculous about this landscape with its squares of green where water from automatic sprinklers performs graceful dances and scatters its life-giving freshness, while in the distance lies the empty expanse of sand and nothingness.

'The end of the world' is what the pioneers of Neot Hakikar call their isolated little farming community. In this small forgotten corner at the furthermost point of the Negev (founded only a few years ago by a mixed bunch of 'dreamers') dwell ingrained idealists, disappointed lovers, and those whom life has maimed, all desperately seeking to find a new meaning and a new life far away from the boundaries of the frenetic world outside.

'The first time I went to Neot Hakikar I thought the people there were crazy!' David Ben Gurion, whose words these were, has exemplified the desert life to a whole generation by abandoning the padded ministerial salons in Jerusalem in order to tend his gardens in Sde Boker in the Negev.

Palm-grove in the Negev (*above*)   Plantations on the Yotvata kibbutz (*below*)

Overleaf: The Negev – cultivation in the middle of **desert land**

Arad

Ein Bokek

Beersheba

Arad, Beersheba, Dimona, Kiryat Gat – these mushroom towns share the same history. They have grown up in the heart of the desert, white, modern and functional, all looking slightly unfinished, which is a trait of an ever-changing Negev.

These cities grew too swiftly through sheer necessity. First of all tiny concrete blocks were built haphazardly under the pinkish sun. Then the greenery came; business started in a small way; and so wide avenues were cut. But at the end of these still lies the desert sand . . .

Beersheba is the ancient patriarchal city where Abraham came to water his herds and Moses to look for a wife. It owes its name (meaning 'well of the oath') to the alliance formed between the Philistine king Abimelech and the first monotheist. The Bible tells us 'there they sware both of them'.

Until 1948 when the battle of the Negev took place and the state of Israel was founded, Beersheba was the only town in the district with a large Arab population. In just a few years it has changed from a poor and arid settlement into an economic and cultural centre, the favourite spot for Jews from North Africa.

The young sabarim came to settle in Arad, the newest town in the Negev, and it rapidly became a university centre. For them this marriage with the desert is the second breath of Zionism. Many students come here from abroad to rediscover 'their paternal language', as the poet Claude Vigée puts it.

Dimona, halfway between Beersheba and Sdom, was started in 1955 to provide housing for employees in the Dead Sea factories. There are whispers that it is here that Israel is secretly preparing its future defence programme . . .

Ein Bokek, near the Dead Sea is known for its hot sulphur springs. But these desert towns, Beersheba excepted, have very little history, though they make up for this deficiency with their youthful dynamism and ever-growing populations. Doubtless the material and fiscal advantages given them by the government have something to do with this but the people also have an inexhaustible supply of idealism, the secret of the Negev's new life.

Ben Gurion recounts how the young **Sde Boker** pioneers told him they had given up armed combat in favour of taming the desert. 'The young people said, "If the Nabataeans could live here once then we can live here today." And so I asked them "Can I join you?" They looked astonished but made no objections. I resigned from office at the end of 1953 and came to Sde Boker.'

Timna – King Solomon's mines

Sculpture at Mitzpeh Ramon

On the Arava road leading to Eilat you should stop at Timna where **King Solomon's mines** are to be found. The Bible tells us that in this valley of smiths, dominated by a huge spur of reddish rock columns, King Solomon employed tens of thousands of slaves working the mines and smelting the copper, about 1,000 years before Christ. Legend says that in biblical times the breeze would softly blow the fires of King Solomon's mines 'like the bellows in a forge'. Today the Israelis tear the riches out of the valley's depths.

It was from Etzion Geber (present-day Eilat) that ships of the old Jewish kingdom used to carry their merchandise to the African countries and return full of 'gold, silver, ivory, monkeys and parrots'. And it was also at Etzion Geber that the Queen of Sheba landed when she came to pay her famous visit to the writer of the Song of Songs.

For centuries the sea of sand in the Negev has covered the remains of splendid fortresses carved to endure in Jewish history. The rocks are silent here; they give no clue as to past events. Here and there, however, there are gaping wounds in the earth – such as the Makhtesh Ramon at **Mitzpeh Ramon** – under which whole cities were buried in times gone by.

The picturesque setting of Mitzpeh Ramon

The small town of Mitzpeh Ramon with its wooden huts is insignificant in itself. The main road in the south, built along the Arava plain, ignores it completely. But the countryside here is some of the most impressive in the Negev; it is no less than a huge museum where nature is imitating art, a huge maze of rock faces seeming to writhe in convulsions, with winding hairpin roads.

It was on the plateau of Mitzpeh Ramon (890 metres high) that Moses had to face the rebellious Hebrew defeatists who yearned for 'the fish which we did eat in Egypt freely'.

Underwater at Eilat

Eilat

During the lifetime of the Kingdom of Judea the port of Etzion Geber was coveted constantly by neighbouring powers, because it was the beginning of the spice route and the seagoing highway to Africa and the Far East.

Today the port of **Eilat** gives the state of Israel a window opening on to Africa, a porthole through which this isolated and once more proscribed people can calmly view the horizon.

But Eilat is also a pure and transparent sea full of colourful fish and magnificent **coral islands** facing the town. It is a holiday beach with brand-new hotels, leisure facilities and tourists who come from all four corners of the earth. Sometimes swimmers from Israel can wave in the sea to swimmers from Jordan who have come over from the beach at Aqaba.

And for the world's hippies Eilat has become a second Katmandu. In summer they are legion, globe-trotters or bohemians. If the hotels depended on them for custom they would go bankrupt – they all sleep out under the stars at the water's edge!

The Gulf of Aqaba

7

Sinai

'This is the mountain where God chose to live.'
Berechit Raba

At the dawn of their history the Hebrews had their experience of the desert and in their wanderings they often touched the bounds of the sublime and the absolute. 'I recalled the gracefulness of youth, the love of our betrothal day, when you followed me to the desert, into an unfruitful land.' This cry of the Prophet illustrates how acutely **Sinai** is at the core of the collective memory of the Jewish people. The doctors of the law go even further, saying that every Jew should consider himself as having been present in person in Sinai at the time of the Revelation.

For it is here that the mystic, turbulent and passionate marriage of God and Israel and their historic meeting took place.

This desert has to be engraved for all time on the hearts and minds of the Jews. Freed from the organized civilisation of the Pharoahs' Egypt, the Hebrews went there first of all to rid themselves of the physical taints and mental alienation of the years of slavery. On the edge of Sinai God commanded his rediscovered people to go in search of their soul, to recover their order and true values . . . This was to last for 40 years, time enough for the generation who had grown up in slavery to give way to men who were free to make their own decisions.

Sinai was, then, not only a place to be crossed but also *the* place of birth, growth and resurrection for a people who had been debased by the exile in Egypt and who now rediscovered the forgotten words of the age-old promise.

The true significance of this 'crossing of the desert' and the 'return to the desert' was felt strongly by the later prophets such as Elijah who withdrew into Sinai to bathe in the original springs of Israel's faith.

The Sinai desert is the one place on earth where one looks beyond the things of this world to the essential and the absolute. A legend of the Talmud tells how the Torah was given out publicly and in daylight, in a place owned by no man, so that 'whoever desires to receive it should come and accept it'.

The solitude and silence which prevail here bring one face to face with God. In Hebrew 'midbar' (desert) comes from the same root as 'word' so that the principles of the Hebrew language underline the correlation between the desert and the word – it was, of course, on Sinai that the word of God was revealed.

Ever since the Revelation poets and hermits have come into this lifeless, breathless wasteland to confront God and to discover themselves.

By the terms of the peace treaty signed between Israel and Egypt in March 1979, the Israelis evacuated El Arish and Atur in May 1979. In December 1979 the Israelis will evacuate Sinai up to a 'line' between El Arish in the North and Ras Mohammed in the South. In March 1982 it is planned that the Israelis shall evacuate the remainder of Sinai and create a new border stretching from Gaza to Eilat.

The Sinai desert

Overleaf:
Mount Sinai
and the Monastery of St. Catherine

Maris which crosses Gaza to Cantara; the peninsula from Beersheba to the Canal; and the pilgrims' way which used to take Arab believers to Mecca and Medina.

Apart from **the desert of 'three days without water'** of which the Bible speaks, the peninsula does not resemble the traditional sandy plain of softly undulating dunes. The Sinai desert contains graceless white hills and sheer and imposing mountains, crumpled and compressed by the erosion of the waves of white stinging sand from the tussocks of dried grass.

Iridescent red and pink porphyry, greyish gneiss, milky quartz and bluish steel all flash in the gold and copper sun, giving the mountains their peculiar beauty, and inviting men to gather their riches.

The peninsula is dominated by the three highest peaks – Jebel Musa (2,224 metres), Jebel Catherina (2,602 metres) and Jebel Serbal (2,053 metres) – rising over a cracked and painful landscape. At the foot of Jebel Musa crouches the Monastery of St. Catherine. The true Mount Sinai of the Bible is, however, identified with Jebel Serbal to the northwest.

The Hebrews left no holy relics in Sinai: this was not a permanent dwelling place for them, only their birthplace. Moreover, Jewish tradition does not admit sacred stones. Time and the word, or silence and memory, make these places holy in their eyes. Throughout their wanderings the Hebrews carried the Ark of the Covenant in a simple tent made of skins before a temple was built to house it in Jerusalem. It was in this desert too that the Hebrew people learned to feel the sense of eternity and immanence which helped them through the whole of their exile.

A few charred carcasses of lorries and armed cars lie rusting under the merciless sun. Sinai is a huge, inhospitable and lifeless triangle of some 60,000 square kilometres, a bloodless, arid land stirred only by raiding parties, Arab horsemen and modern warfare.

This desert has always been a meeting-place between Africa and Asia and ambitions and jealousies were further roused by the construction of the Suez Canal. Three large gashes run through it, like veins, from end to end – the sea-route, the old Via

The desert of 'three days without water' of the Bible

El Arish palm-grove

In the Sinai desert the Hebrew wanderers from beyond the frontiers learned how to entwine two civilisations, two sorts of people, two ways of life. For 2,000 years of exile these children of the word have been forced into a nomadic existence, carrying with them a moral courage that should enrich the world and its history: 2,000 years, the longest 'crossing of the desert' that a race has ever accomplished.

The lack of water in Sinai caused the Hebrews to reproach Moses, their leader. The only large oasis is Pharan and nowadays **the El Arish palm-grove** (now in Egypt as it was evacuated by the Israelis in May 1979) welcomes the Bedouins under its benevolent shade. Scholars have identified this spot as the biblical Succa. Many conquerors, including Alexander Jannaeus, Napoleon and the British army have sought to control this vital watering-place with its majestic and indolently-waving palms.

But the masters of the place, **the Sinai Bedouins**, have a relationship some thousand years old with the spot. They scorn the assaults of tourist industry and petrol-driven transport. Today they still continue to practise their own almost forgotten lifestyle – that of always being at liberty to move on . . .

Sinai Bedouins

Miniature on the episcopal chair representing the Monastery of St. Catherine

When it was first built **the Monastery of St. Catherine**, crouching under the mass of Jebel Musa, was nothing more than a precarious retreat for hermits and pilgrims. It was fortified and turned into a watchtower during its occupations and subsequent reoccupations by different religious groups. In the year 527 the Sinai hermits begged the Emperor Justinian for his protection after plunderers had destroyed the monastery and he ordered his architect, Elisha, to build a fortress in place of the old Tower of the Burning Bush. Elisha was executed once the work was finished – he had built the fortress at the foot of the mountain when Justinian wanted it at the top!

Justinian's fortifications were built from granite blocks, in the Byzantine tradition, but today only the southern section, known as the Mountain Wall, remains. The rest was restored and rebuilt at various times by General Kléber acting under orders from Napoleon.

An underground passage hollowed out under the parvis allows access to a splendid garden without having to leave the monastery. The main door, called Bab el Rais, through which the archbishops used to pass on their return from Jerusalem, has been bricked up since 1722. There is an inscription on it in Greek, 'This is the doorway to Eternal Life through which the Just Men will pass'.

St. Catherine's Church has a central nave flanked by two side aisles and several chapels. The western Narthex door is decorated in the simple Coptic style with sculptured panels.

The Monastery of St. Catherine seen from St. Catherine's Mount

In front of the choir is the basilica's iconostasis which has two registers of paintings. St. Catherine's harbours an astonishingly rich collection of icons, numbering about 5,000. The monastery's connections with many other countries meant that some of these portable works of art were exchanged with other monasteries. Others would suggest that they had been painted here, because of the similarity in their treatment and in their depiction of monks and bishops practising in the monastery. That there were studios of artists and copyists here, as there were in many of the larger monasteries, is borne out by the sketches hanging on the wall of the Theotokos chapel next door to the old library, and by the close resemblance in style between certain of the icons and the **miniatures** in the library manuscripts.

Portable icons earlier than the period of the Macedonian emperors and the Comnenes had long been given up for lost until it was discovered that this

The Nativity, a post-Byzantine icon

The Monastery of St. Catherine – a pastoral scene, a gospel miniature

old monastery had been spared in the iconoclasm because it was cut off from the Byzantine state by the Arab occupation.

The very **early Christian encaustic icons** date from the foundation of the sanctuary in Justinian's time and are the sole surviving examples of the sixth century art of Syria and Egypt. They were painted on relatively thin board and the colours were mixed with wax and applied to the wood without a previous covering of plaster. They have thus retained an astonishing freshness and transparency.

Apart from the portraits of holy men and women typical of the old art of icon painting, the subjects are all taken from the Gospels or from dogma – the 12 festivals, the miracles, Christ's life and Passion, the saints and martyrs. The scenes and the people in the icons and **mosaics** are elevated from earthly life by the touches of gold-leaf on the clothes and backgrounds, which create an air of unreality. The art of icon painting in the **post-Byzantine period** is

The Virgin and Child, an eleventh century mosaic

more closely allied to that of the miniaturist with strong bright colours and superimposed scenes confined in a limited space.

Before the monks began their work they used to spend three days in prayer and fasting so that their paintings would reflect, in some small measure, the depths of their inner life in the Byzantine tradition.

St. Peter, an encaustic icon of the sixth century   137

Monastery of St. Catherine
Mohammed's Charter

Monastery of St. Catherine
Bonaparte's Charter

Despite the importance of these icons, ancient as their creation was in the silent confines of the monastery, they are, nevertheless, not as precious as the faded manuscripts, aged scrolls, gospels and psalters on show in the monastery library. (Incidentally, this library is the most famous and ancient monastery library known.)

There are some 3,300 historical manuscripts here, including the Codex Sinaiticus, a seventeen centuries-old translation of the Bible and, of particular note, the Akd Name, **Mohammed's Charter** and the Sinai Orders or **Bonaparte Charter**.

Mohammed's Charter is a decree initialled by Mohammed himself, who is reputed to have once received the hospitality of the St. Catherine's monks. The Charter commands 'the faithful of Islam to help the Sinai monastery, to allow the monks there to worship and serve God freely according to their own religion, and to exempt them from all bondage and taxes.'

The monastery of St. Catherine was given official protection by the Muslim chief, Caliph Omar, who occupied the Sinai peninsula in 634. But the Arabs did not take much notice of the Akd Name or its conditions and the monastery was frequently looted and the monks killed. It was only after Bonaparte's campaign in Palestine that St. Catherine's enjoyed the official protection of the French army. The conditions of Mohammed's Charter were almost identical with the Sinai Orders of Bonaparte and Kléber, 'The holy men should be allowed to govern themselves in this place and the government will prevent them from being disturbed in their worship'.

Legends are long-lived at St. Catherine's. Among them is the legend of Catherine herself, daughter of the king of Alexandria. She was martyred because of her decision to become a convert to Christianity and her relics are preserved in a white marble sarcophagus behind the iconostasis. Another legend says that this is the very spot where Moses had the vision of the Burning Bush. Today the semi-circular apse in **the Chapel of the Burning Bush** contains one of the monastery's most precious mosaics – the fresco of the Transfiguration of Christ.

'The dwelling-place of solitude surrounded by the desert' was how Pierre Loti described the Monastery of St. Catherine, and never has a definition better described such a spot.

The 'Burning Bush' and, on the right, the apse of the Chapel of the Burning Bush

In the course of centuries many chapels were built in and around the monastery. **The Mount Sinai Chapel** was built as a hermitage where men could cut themselves off from the world to attain purity.

Judaism does not hold with such cutting oneself off from history. This was one of the important lessons learnt by the Jewish people in their desert encounter with the Universal.

'There were thunders and lightenings and a thick cloud upon the mount and the voice of the trumpet exceeding loud.' This is the description given in the Bible of the moment of Revelation so passionately awaited by a whole race. Moses came back from his personal encounter with God to give his people a law which was to overturn their lives and make them 'a people who cannot be thought of amongst the nations'. At the same time the course of history was changed.

Did the Jews really accept this alliance which was to make them a sacerdotal community with good grace, as the unanimous cry, 'We shall perform then we shall understand', would suggest? Or was it a case of, 'so stubborn that God threw down Mount Sinai like a cooking-pot and would not lift the lid again until the people had accepted the law', which is how the rabbinical story goes?

Whichever way it was, the Jew experienced a painful liberty, in fear and trembling, here in the desert. He accepted the role of a people 'that pitches its tent among the nations'; accepted a life at once part of, yet separate from, the rest of the world.

The echo from Sinai and the remembrance of the bond which joined the people, Moses, the law and God all helped to perpetuate the unwearying memory of Israel in the later exiles. It was a memory fed neither by feats of arms nor glorious works of art but only by their adherence to the word of God.

Mount Sinai was the birthplace of the vocation of this race that 'calls men together to glorify Jerusalem and at the same time the world' (André Neher). Israel – a name of destiny! The word means both 'he who fights against God' and 'he who walks straight towards God'. This is the essential ambiguity of the destiny of a people that has fought against God, then with God, and finally for God, but never totally without him.

The Talmud says that Israel has been compared both to the dust and the stars. 'When they lower themselves they touch the dust of the ground: when they raise themselves they reach to the stars'.

And Yehuda Halevy, greatest of the mediaeval Hebrew poets and philosophers, adds this thought: 'Israel compared to other nations is as the heart at the centre of the body – at once the sickest and the healthiest of all the organs.'

appendix

Moses receiving the Tables of the Law, an icon of Damaskinos

1 · Israel and its History

THE PEOPLE IN PALESTINE

Abraham and the Patriarchs

The history of the Jewish people begins with the patriach Abraham obeying the Divine Voice telling him to leave his native land and go to Canaan: 'Get thee out of thy country . . . unto a land that I will shew thee. And I will make of thee a great nation . . . and in thee shall all familics of the earth be blessed'.

Abraham, who is rightly considered as the founder of the Jewish people, fathered Isaac who, at the end of his life, was unable to prevent the split between his two sons, Jacob and Esau.

God was to make Jacob his chosen ally. The alliance was sealed in the combat with the angel and after his victory over this divine messenger, Jacob took on the name of Israel. He then went down into Egypt where he and his children settled, because the land of Canaan was stricken by famine.

Moses and the Judges

Jacob's children and grandchildren lived for many years in Egypt. There the children of Israel were persecuted and then forced into slavery. From that time forth they were united in their hatred for the country of the pharoahs and in their spiritual idealisation of their ever-remembered ancestors. When an Israelite called Moses, who had been raised (by a combination of circumstances) in the royal court, incited them to open rebellion under the divine banner, the Jewish people rose as one and followed him. In about 1445 BC he led his people out of Egypt towards the borders of the Promised Land, which he himself was never to know. During the 40 years of Exodus in the desert, however, he had instilled high moral values into his people and had handed over the precious tablets of the law to them.

The long and painful struggle to conquer Canaan was led by Moses' successor, Joshua. After the siege of Jericho and an interminable war, the country was divided among the 12 tribes of the Jewish people. When Joshua died each tribe appointed its own leader, called a 'Judge' but very soon the Hebrews came to realise that only if the tribes were united under one king could they protect their country which was under constant attack from its neighbours.

First representation of the word 'shalom' (peace)

The Kings

The prophet Samuel anointed Saul, a country boy from the tribe of Benjamin, as king of Israel. From then on the land of Canaan became a monarchy. After Saul came David, the slayer of the giant Goliath: then his son, Solomon, the wisest of rulers and author of the Song of Songs, who built the Temple of God in Jerusalem. When Solomon died in 930 the kingdom split into Judah and Israel. Jeremiah, who deplored the corruption of royal power, the perversion of the priesthood, the idolatry and sin which began to be rife, predicted that one day the country would 'vomit forth its inhabitants'.

Exile, restoration and domination

Jeremiah's terrible prophecy camc true. First the kingdom of Israel was annexed by the Assyrians in 722 BC. Then Nebuchadnezzar destroyed the temple in Jerusalem after laying siege to the city in 587 BC. The end finally came for the kingdom of Judah when thousands of Jews were deported to Babylon.

After some 50 years in exile the Persian Cyrus eventually allowed the Jews to come back to their own country and rebuild their temple.

While this construction was going on the Jews who had been scattered throughout the Persian Empire escaped a massacre planned by the minister Aman, thanks to Queen Esther who interceded for them with Assuerus.

Persian domination finally ended and Alexander of Macedon was the next conqueror of the country. When his empire was divided Palestine returned to the Seleucids. Jews were again persecuted

The star of David

The menorah

during the reign of Antiochus Epiphanes and then came the heroic rising of the Hasmoneans, the family of high priests who led the revolt and freed the country. From then on the country was independent and was ruled by a 'Nasi' and a 'Sanhedrin' (the Greek word for a court of justice).

But the freedom of Hasmonean rule only lasted for 80 years. In 63 BC Pompey seized Jerusalem and the Jews were once more forced to suffer at the whims of foreign domination – this time it was the Romans. Again they tried to throw off the yoke. John of Galilee and Simon Bar-Ghiora led the zealot revolt but this merely resulted in the siege of Jerusalem and the destruction of the second temple. The name of Titus, the Roman emperor who took the Holy City in 70 BC and

sacked the temple, joined that of Nebuchadnezzar in the sad memories of the exiled Jews.

The last struggles of Jewish nationalism, in the Bar Kokhba revolt, were strangled at birth.

From then on the country came under merciless Roman domination, which became even harder for the Hebrews when Christianity was made the offical religion after the conversion of Constantine. The Roman Empire was divided in 395 and Palestine then found itself part of the Byzantine Empire, suffering a heavy and oppressive rule which lasted more than two centuries. The Arab invaders were welcomed as they were more lenient and in 639 Caliph Omar took Jerusalem. But Christian Europe would not allow Christ's tomb to remain in the hand of the infidels and in 1099 the Crusaders led by Godefroy de Bouillon occupied Jerusalem and created the kingdom of Jerusalem. This kingdom was short-lived and was destroyed in 1187 by Saladin, the Sultan of Egypt. A few Frankish fiefs remained, as did a number of strongholds manned by Knights Templar and Hospitallers. When Saint John of Acre fell in 1291 these last outposts slipped from the Crusaders' grasp and Palestine became subject to the

Egyptian dynasty of the Mamelukes. In 1517 the country was conquered by the Turks who occupied it until 1918 when the British succeeded the Ottomans.

THE DIASPORA

The Diaspora (dispersion) dates from even before the end of biblical times. At the time when the Roman Empire was in decline Jews were already scattered throughout Europe and North Africa.

When Christianity took root in the western Roman Empire the Jews began to experience the misery of forced conversion, hatred and persecution. In 589 Spain forbade the practising of the Jewish faith and compelled Jews to adopt the Christian religion. What was called the 'golden age' of the Exile only dawned when the Arabs conquered Spain in 711–714.

The tolerance which Islam showed towards the Jewish people is unique in the annals of the Hebrews.

In the thirteeeth century the long struggle between Christians and Muslims over who would conquer Spain ended in a victory for the Christians. The new Spanish princes may have given pause for thought to the useful Jewish contribution to the country's development, but religious fanaticism proved stronger. In spite of renewed persecution the community continued to flourish, but gradually the Church's latent hatred showed itself again. The end of the fourteenth century was the era of Torquemada's Inquisition, resulting in false conversions, arrests, torture and the condemnation of the Jews as being guilty of Christ's death. In 1492, two centuries after the Jews had been driven out of England, Ferdinand of Aragon and Isabella of Castile signed an edict which ordered all Jews to leave Spain within three months. It was a sad end for the idyll of Judaism in Spain.

The greatest Jewish centre in the Middle Ages, apart from Spain, was Germany. It was this separate development which gave rise to the divisions of Sephardi and Ashkenazi. The persecution of the Ashkenazi Jews began in the twelfth century, much earlier than that of their fellow worshippers in Spain. Beyond the Rhine Jews were restricted to certain jobs and confined in their own strictly segregated districts, the ghettos. The Yiddish dialect was cultivated in all these communities and became the means of communication between Ashkenazi Jews.

Then in the sixteenth century Poland took the place of Germany as the rallying point for European Jews. The Jewish community in Poland and Lithuania became rich and prosperous. It enjoyed unrestricted development and produced that spirit of adventure which engendered hassidism, a movement mid-way between mysticism and epicureanism.

In September 1797 France became the first country to liberate the Jews from their secular servitude, when the Assembly passed a law granting Jews the same civil rights as Christians. The ripples were to spread to Holland, Italy and further afield.

Russia annexed the Polish lands with their million-odd Jews at the end of the eighteenth century. The Tsars ordered regular pogroms to strengthem their tottering regime and so the great emigration of Russian Jews to America and Palestine began in 1881 and 1882.

Theodor Herzl

THE RETURN

Zionism and the beginnings of immigration

The anti-semitism which spread through western Europe at the end of the nineteenth century, the bloodthirsty pogroms in Russia, the rise of the spirit of nationalism in the world at large . . . all these factors favoured the birth of a movement which crystallized latent aspirations and longings into a political and sociological expression – Zionism.

Theodor Herzl published *The Jewish State* in 1895. The young Jewish journalist had gone to 'cover' the Dreyfus affair in Paris, had discovered anti-semitism and so had decided to devote his life to the renaissance of his people. Before him philosophers such as Lilienblum, Pinsker and Ahad Haam would discuss the questionable Jewish emancipation in the Diaspora and theorise about 'auto-emancipation', national renewal and a rediscovering of Jewish roots.

Political Zionism took its first steps under the aegis of Theodor Herzl in 1897. At Basle in Switzerland the first Zionist Congress united all 'Lovers of Zion' and declared they would 'establish Jewish organisations everywhere to strengthen the people's awareness of themselves and to get governments to support the goals of Zionism.' The BILU, the first colonists from Russia, began to settle in Palestine, supported by various organisations and, in particular, by Baron Edmond de Rothschild in Paris.

At the same time as Zionist enthusiasm was stirring the Jewish masses in Russia to envisage a future Jewish state, other Jews there were taking a leading role in the coming revolution. The Union of Jewish workers in Russia and Poland, formed in 1897, was fighting for national

1909: the future site of Tel Aviv

rights in the future socialist republic.

Towards the end of the First World War Dr. Chaim Weizmann succeeded in obtaining a declaration from Great Britain of their support for the establishment of Palestine as a 'national home' for the Jewish people. This famous Balfour Declaration of 2nd November 1917 was the first major victory for Zionism.

The Aliyah (immigration) of pioneers began to get under way. Colonies, villages, kibbutzim and towns grew up and were reborn and first clashes with the Arab inhabitants had already degenerated into the occasional bloody battle.

Great Britain, who had been given the Mandate for Palestine by the League of Nations in 1922 after the Peace Conference at Versailles, struggling to be impartial decided to stem the flow of Jewish immigration.

The Second World War

In May 1939, on the eve of what was to be the most horrifying phenomenon in European Jewish history, with Hitler already showing his claws, the British government decided virtually to close the gates to Palestine. The Government White Paper authorised no more than 75,000 Jews to settle in Israel. This raised a general outcry from the Jewish Agency and David Ben Gurion passionately declared 'We will fight against war as if there were no White Paper and the White Paper as if there were no war'. From then on the Yishuv openly opposed the Mandatory Power and the Haganah and the Irgun, two independent resistance groups, were formed.

Birth of a State

In 1947 Great Britain brought the Palestine question before the United Nations and on 29th November the General Assembly voted to partition Palestine into two independent states, one Arab, the other Jewish. Henceforth the Jews would have a homeland.

But the State of Israel had scarcely been born before the Arabs refused. This refusal was to lead to three wars and make a country whose true calling was peace into a land of 'fire and blood'.

David Ben Gurion proclaiming the creation of the state of Israel on 14th May 1948

2 · Advice to tourists

Israel might not be the complete 'Jewish hotel' that Ben Gurion once jokingly called it, but it is a very fertile ground for a unique social experience, where you can encounter people and languages from all corners of the earth. You should not only visit it for its Holy Places and historical sites, but also savour the community life of its cafés, its buses (something is always going on on an Israeli bus!), its synagogues and markets. The diversity of the faces and backgrounds of Israel today is more rewarding than its relics from ancient history.

Transport: it is easy to get around in a country as narrow as Israel. The most interesting way is to 'tramp' (hitch-hike) and if you don't want to be spotted as a tourist immediately, then don't use your thumb, point downwards with your index finger!

Train – there is a northern line between Jerusalem, Tel-Aviv, Haifa, and Nahariya, and a southern line to Beersheba and Dimona. It is rather shaky, but if you have the time it does provide a slower and more detailed view of the country. Don't be surprised if you see men muttering as they try to keep their balance on the train in the evenings – they are praying!

The national bus network, run by the Egged company is very comprehensive and runs regular services to all places of interest in Israel. A special go-where-you-please tourist pass is available at a fixed price and is valid for a fortnight. The company also organises tourist trips with commentaries from guides who are frequently experts and always volunteers.

The 'national institution' as far as transport is concerned in Israel is the *sherut* (a communal taxi with seats for seven passengers). These go from town to town at fairly reasonable prices. You may have the 'privilege' of witnessing the horde of tricks the Israelis employ to get themselves the front seat!

The Arkia company runs internal flights to Eilat, Sinai and Sharm-e-Sheikh which may be preferable to the exhausting and rambling bus journeys, though less picturesque.

1. Tel Aviv and the North Coast

Tel Aviv: your first experience here is often the exotic central bus and taxi station (Tahana Hamerkazit), but you should be quick if you wish to see it as it is to be replaced by an ultramodern coach station. What this will gain in hygiene it will lose in character!

A town is rarely so well designed as this, for strolling about in as the fancy takes one. Even the inhabitants show a bohemian free-and-easiness which makes them look like tourists in their own streets. 'In Tel Aviv you enjoy yourself, in Haifa you work and in Jerusalem you pray . . .'

Ben Yehuda Street, Hayarkon Street and, especially, Dizengoff Street are the centre of Tel Aviv's night-life and are full of restaurants, cafes, art galleries, boutiques, discotheques and cinemas. Pop music fans should visit Tiffany's in the Dan Hotel.

Jaffa: try and visit Jaffa at night. Don't loiter in the art galleries or the craft shops, because prices are astronomical! It is wiser to stop in the taverns and taste the grills washed down with *arac*, or fruit juice.

As you leave Tel Aviv you can follow the coast southwards and stop at Ashdod, a new city full of North African immigrants and the future major port of Israel.

If you go northwards you can bathe on the beaches of Tel Aviv's residential suburbs or at Herzliya (there is a private pool in the Akadia Hotel). Stop at the small French-Algerian run cafes and terrace gardens in Natanya for kebabs.

Caesarea: visit the amphitheatre. In August there are cultural activities (theatre, open-air concerts etc.). The marble columns on the beach are worth making a detour to see.

Saint John of Acre: visit Jezzar Pasha's mosque, the Municipal Museum in the ancient Sultan's bath, the fortifications, St. John's Church and its crypt. You should save the afternoon for a wander through the bazaar and try your hand at the subtle techniques of bargaining – even though it is a game which the tourist always loses!

Go on as far as Rosh Hanikra and its picturesque views (accessible by cable-car). This is the last outpost of Israel at the frontier with Lebanon.

Haifa: you should visit Hadar Hacarmel, the business centre, the Institute of Technology campus and the Municipal Museum. The Bahaist temple has wonderful walks in its Persian gardens. You should also look out over the bay from Mount Carmel (preferably when it is lit up at night) before going down for a wander around old Haifa in the vicinity of the port.

It is better to visit Haifa at the end of the week since there are less religious restrictions observed here on the Sabbath because of its socialist tendencies (it is known as the 'red' city).

Outside Haifa there are excursions to the artists' village of Ein Hod and to Beit Shearim, the necropolis of the Talmudic sages. You can arrange all your trips around high and low Galilee here in Haifa.

2. Galilee and the North

Nazareth: a key spot for Christian pilgrims. Visit the Church and the Grotto of the Annunciation, St. Joseph's house and the Virgin's fountain. If you have time take a bus round the new Jewish quarter of Nazareth Illit and see the original and striking design of the synagogue there. A wander round the Arab souk is virtually a 'must'.

Take a trip to Cana, five miles from Nazareth and visit the Greek and Franciscan churches there.

Tiberias: contains several synagogues and rabbis' tombs. Water ski-ing, sailing and supervised bathing-places on the lake. Plenty of refreshment facilities – particularly fish and chips!

Excursions go to Capernaum; the Hot Springs and Rabbi Meir Baal Haness' tomb; the Ein Gev kibbutz, the El Hamma springs.

On the way from Tiberias to Safad make a detour to the Mount of the Beatitudes.

Safad: holiday resort with numerous and comfortable hotels. Visit the 'Ari' synagogue. Artists' quarter (the old Arab quarter). From Safad you can go out to Meiron, two and a half miles away, to see the tomb of Rabbi Shimon bar Yochai, author of the Zohar.

While in Galilee you should also see Dan and the source of the River Jordan and also visit one of the many kibbutzim in the area, perhaps Degania – the first of them all.

From Galilee you can 'go up' to Jerusalem either by the new lands or via Tel Aviv and the Sharon Valley.

3.–4. Jerusalem

On leaving Tel Aviv watch for the Mikveh Israel Agricultural School (over 100 years old). Halfway to Jerusalem, in *Ramla*, take a quick look at the Ottoman tower. Detours are worthwhile to the abbey at Latrun, to Abu Ghosh (a charming Arab Village), to Kiryat Anavim and to the park at Aqua Bella (camping site).

You really need twice as much time to discover Jerusalem. The old city must take precedence and should be visited quarter by quarter – Jewish, Christian, Muslim – taking in all the places of pilgrimage and the monuments. Each stage will take at least half a day. Devote the afternoons to the souks and one evening to the *son et lumière* show at David's Tower. At any hour of the day or night you can find people praying at the Wailing Wall. There are lots of reasonably-priced restaurants in the Arab town (such as the Golden Chicken, Massouada, Caves du Roy). Have an ice-cream at the Metzuda (the citadel) outside the walls near the Jaffa gate.

In the new city visit the Kyria, the Knesset, the National Museum and the university on the same day. Lunch in one of the university's cafeterias, then why not siesta on the campus lawns?

Don't miss tasting *falafel*, *schwama* (doner kebab) and *shishkebab* off the open-air stalls. Eat casually at the Taamon, or more formally at the Alno and the Atara.

The two best known restaurants are Finks and Chez Simon (expensive but authentic French cooking). Be sure to sample the *humus* at Taami's (a good and popular place to eat).

If you can, stroll around the Mea Shearim district on the eve of the Sabbath (respectably dressed) and go into one of the synagogues.

But above all, wander round Jerusalem as the fancy takes you and drink in the sounds and the colours and the people.

5. Judea and Samaria

Bethlehem: visit the Church and the Grotto of the Nativity, St. Catherine's Church and the Shepherds' Field, as well as Rachel's Tomb.

A walk around the affluent suburb of Beit Jala is recommended.

Hebron: visit to the Machpelah Tomb.

Nablus (the old Schechem): climb Mount Guerzim where you may meet with some Samaritans.

Masada: the rock can be reached by cable-car. It is worth the effort, though, to climb up on foot early in the morning (at four or five o'clock).

For relaxation, don't spend too long on the shores of the Dead Sea but rather go on to the small oasis of Ein Gedi.

Jericho: spend a welcome day in this oasis of coolness in the Judean desert. Visit the remains of Herod's Jericho. There is a swimming pool at the Springs of Elisha. Excursions to the convent of St. John the Baptist, then on towards the Place of Baptism on the Jordan. Visit the excavations at Khirbet Mefjer.

6. The Negev and the Red Sea

Beersheba: a new town despite its age-old history. Nothing of particular interest to tourists, apart from the desert reclamation and the picturesque Bedouin market.

Sdom: lies approximately 400 metres below sea-level. Take traditional photographs of bathing in the Dead Sea and the salt statue of Lot's wife.

New immigrant towns worth seeing are Dimona and Arad.

Eilat: difficult to 'survive' more than a day in the stifling atmosphere (unless you are a hippy!). Depending on how fit you are you can sleep on the beach, in a youth hostel, in an air-conditioned hotel or a private guest house. Underwater swimming and glass-bottom boat trips to the coral island. Visit to the 'fjord'. The water is warm enough for all-year-round bathing.

At Neot Hakikar unusual rambles are organised by the local inhabitants (a group of idealists and lay-prophets!) along their mysterious tracks through the Negev desert.

7. Sinai

Transport is difficult in Sinai and it is best to join an organised excursion to El Arish then to the Monastery of St. Catherine and Mount Sinai.

You can travel by air or by bus to the up-and-coming holiday centre of Sharme-Sheikh.

3 · Remember . . . . .

If you want to travel in Israel bear in mind that the Israelis are a warm, hospitable race and will be only too pleased to chat to you (in any language!) and to help you to organise visits or meetings.

Whenever you go into public places, shops or a private house, or when you meet friends in the street, it is customary to use the greeting 'Shalom' (peace) and on Saturday 'Shabbat Shalom' (peaceful Sabbath).

As soon as you arrive in the country you have to get used to the lack of activity on the Sabbath. On Friday evenings everything stops as soon as the first star appears, and difficulties arise for the unsuspecting tourist who wishes to follow a fixed programme. Nothing will start again until Sunday morning. If you want to check out of a 'religious' hotel on Saturday you should pay your bill by four o'clock on Friday so as to avoid complications. In Mea Shearim, the hassidim district of Jerusalem, the observance is so strict that no cars are allowed to be driven there. The Sabbath is best devoted to visiting the Holy Places which are closed on Sundays.

Archaeological sites are open to the public until sunset, but if you wish to visit current excavations you need to approach the Minister for Tourism, 24 Rehov Hamelekh George, Jerusalem.

Be careful to check **the opening times** of the museums because these vary considerably. Generally the rooms are open to the public from 10 a.m. to 1 p.m. and from 4 p.m. to 7 p.m. but some are open on particular evenings. On Friday and Saturday museums close at 1 p.m.

Don't be afraid to use the sheruts (communal taxis) to help you get about. You may even be able to try out your Hebrew in them!

In wintertime you can go from the Galilean Hills, where the temperature is cold, to the subtropical climate on the shores of the Dead Sea and the Red Sea, where there is perpetual summer and you can bathe all year. In the heat of summer you will find the refreshing coolness of Safad particularly welcome.

Veronica ben Yaacov. *After studying in Paris and then in Cambridge, she settled in Israel where she worked for the national radio. Bazak's Guide, the main Israeli tourist guide, asked for her collaboration in selecting and classifying the country's restaurants.*

Restaurants

You can eat well in Israel because the different nationalitites that make up its population each have their own special style of cooking.

First there is the oriental cuisine which is fairly typical of what you will find in any local restaurant. It may be Yemenite, Arab, Tunisian, Moroccan, Greek or Balkan. Then there is western cooking – Polish, Hungarian, Rumanian, Italian and French.

As you travel round the country don't be taken aback to find that Israelis often eat in the street. There are small booths on almost every street corner selling *falafel* (tiny deep-fried balls of chickpeas inside flat Arab *pita* bread) and, in summer, sweet corn on the cob.

Kosher restaurants are preceded by a 'K' in the guide books for practising Jewish tourists. Here the cooking is done according to special rituals: kosher meat (bled) must never be eaten at the same meal as a milk-based dish. The food served in hotels is nearly always kosher.

And now to look at a few restaurants in more detail . . .

In Tel Aviv's Yemenite quarter you will be delighted with the stuffed pigeons or quinces at the Zion Exclusivi restaurant. Or you can dine more cheaply at the Gamliel and Zion. I would advise you to try the Dan Restaurant and the Kispipa for central European dishes. Rumanian cooking might well tempt you with its charcoal grills, aubergines and other specialities. In Jaffa don't forget to pay a visit to Nelu le Veritable at the Ha Amiti as well as the Roi des aubergines. Stop at Lipski's to discover pure Polish cooking, and if you fancy Chinese food, you will be happy at the Singing Bamboo near the old port of Tel Aviv. You will feel the authentic trattoria atmosphere immediately you enter the pizzeria Casa Mia, thanks to its owner, Antonio and his Neapolitan music. For real French cooking go to the Versailles which serves snails and flambé pepper steaks. To fully quench your thirst for European cooking there is still the Casba in the old port of Tel Aviv and the Toutounne in Jaffa. The fish dishes are excellent at Shaldag and Shuster and the journey to Natanya is worth making if only for the *couscous* at Shuv Polet where the Tunisian cooking reaches perfection.

In Haifa you will find the seaside setting of the Misadag fish restaurant at Bat Galim most attractive.

On the way to Tiberias you need only go as far as the Ein Gev kibbutz to enjoy delicious fried fish. In Galilee go and see the American farm and the Vered Ha Galil ranch.

In Jerusalem be sure to go to Alla Gondola for Italian food, to The Mandarin for Chinese, and to Cohen's near Mea Shearim, or Finks, which offer a mixture of Austro-Hungarian food and a well-stocked (but pricey!) bar. During your rambles across the old city you can try Arab cooking at Costas or the Oriental. The French cooking is out of this world at the Relais hippique near Jerusalem airport!

Then if your journey finishes at Eilat, do go to Yoske's – it could well convert you to fishing!

4 · Advice from Israelis

Mrs. Ruth Dayan. *It was by visiting the new immigrant communities that she realised the enormous cultural value brought in by the diverse traditions. This led to her founding and then running Muskit, one of the shops in at the beginning of the amazing development of Israeli craftwork.*

Tradition and crafts

If you like craftwork Israel can offer you a particularly rich mixture of styles combining so many and so varied traditions that it is difficult to cover them adequately here. We really have two distinct divisions: on the one hand the local crafts, which often go back as far as biblical times, such as the old Jewish weaving and dyeing; on the other, the crafts brought in by the many different communities from all parts of the world, all with distinctive traditions, methods and styles.

Individuals tend to do the work as a hobby rather than for a source of income, because of marketing problems and so craft industries have been made more community-orientated in Israel – raffia-work for instance, the potteries in the Druze villages in Carmel, weaving and Yemenite embroidery.

In 1940 Wizo (Women's International Zionist Organisation) started to organise the production and sale of embroidery, lace and leatherwork made by women. But it was really in the fifties that craftwork took off in a big way when immigrants from the East and from North Africa with their own customs, experience and workmanship, caused a greater variation of techniques to develop. Take, as examples, the Gaza carpets which are woven and dyed according to age-old methods; the fine woollen carpets made in the Nazareth workshops and in the Arab villages; the filigree silver jewellery worked by the Yemenites; the embroidery boldly sewn in gold and silver thread by the Bethlehem women who use their own special stitches and colours; the Palestinian embroidery from Gaza with its bright pink, yellow and violet designs and those from Ramla worked in black and red silks; the Moroccan leather and copperwares; the black Gaza pottery, fashioned in underground workshops according to very ancient methods; the blue glass from Hebron and the blown glass of Jerusalem; the olive-wood sculptures as well as the mother-of-pearl work which is the livelihood of a large part of Bethlehem's population.

A new craftsmanship has been born from all these styles, one which has benefited from all the research of these various communities. They continue to work in the places where they live and sell their products through an intermediary such as the central craft organisations Wiso, Maskit and Batsheva.

Wizo has a shop at 87 Allenby Road in Tel Aviv, another in Jerusalem at 34 Jaffa Road, and a third in Haifa at 9 Nordam Street. Both Wizo and Maskit have branches in Natanya, and Batsheva are in Tel Aviv at 32 Ben Yehuda Street and 9 Frey Street.

If you want to find a large number of craft articles or clothes, try the oriental atmosphere of the souk Hapichpechim in Jaffa, and in Jerusalem browse through the large and fascinating bazaar of the oriental towns in the heart of the vaulted alleyways of the old city.

Ori Reisman. *Born on the Tel Joseph kibbutz at Ein Harod, he then studied painting at Tel Aviv and at the Beaux-Arts in Paris. He has been a kibbutznik since the age of 19; since 1949 he has lived on the Kabri kibbutz while taking part in many exhibitions in Israel, Europe and the United States.*

The Kibbutzim

The word kibbutz immediately brings Israel to mind. This form of society was considered ideal right from the time of the Jews returning to Palestine. The variance in the ideologies of socialism and the consequent political choices made, stamp each kibbutz with a different character.

The day begins at 6 a.m. with work in the fields, where the newcomer can easily fit in with the community life and its members. Gradually he will earn the right to choose a type of work more congenial to him in mechanics, perhaps, or joinery or domestic tasks. Family life takes over after siesta-time between five and seven in the evening. Then there is dinner followed by workers' meetings or entertainment which end the very full day.

It is an egalitarian, collectivist society where everything is communal – property, children's education, distribution of income (which is invested in developing and improving the general standard of living). The kibbutz does not solve all an individual's problems but it does offer outsiders the attraction of experiencing a life they feel they might wish for. It can be sampled in one of the following ways –

– a four week minimum stay (for young people between 18 and 30) during which time volunteers must work 36 to 40 hours a week. In return they will receive free accommodation, food, laundry and .pocket money, and at the end of their stay, a one-day sight-seeing tour.
– a 7–28 day holiday in a Kibbutz guest house with the opportunity of touring a Kibbutz.

Information both for this and the previous holiday may be obtained from The Israel Government Tourist Office, 59 St. James's Street, London SW1. Telephone 01–493 2431; or in America, from Israel Government Tourist Office, 350 Fifth Avenue, New York, New York 10001. Telephone (212) 560–0621.

– a six month to a year's stay which allows you to discover fully the good and bad points of a collective existence.

Information can be obtained from Kibbutz Representatives, College House, Finchley Road, London NW3 5ET. Telephone 01–586 4693.

Whichever kibbutz you visit you will immediately be struck by the impression of calmness amid the often unexpected greenery. The kibbutzim devoted to agriculture often have outside interests: they may own guest houses such as those run by Givat Brenner and Shefayim to the north of Tel Aviv, by Beit Oren near Haifa, by Hanita near Rosh Hanikra, by Hagosherim and Tel Hai in Galilee, by Ginnosar on the edge of Lake Tiberias.

The work of artists and researchers is encouraged and I personally, in my role as kibbutz painter, have to give only half the time normally allotted to agricultural work. I devote the rest to painting or to visiting museums and art galleries.

It may be of interest to visit some of our museums –

– the art museum on the Ein Harod kibbutz which exhibits works by kibbutz-movement artists;

Dani Karavan. *From the age of 13 he has been engaged in artistic studies. After spending five years on the kibbutz he then pursued his studies in Florence where he created for the May musical the décor for the 'Consul' of Menotti. A sculptor, a painter, a gifted artist in many fields, he is one of the outstanding personalities in contemporary art.*

– the museums of the survivors from the ghettos on the Lohamei Hageitaot and Yad Mordechai kibbutzim;
– the museum of prehistory at Sha'ar Hagolan where many local discoveries are on show and the archeological museums of Nir David, Ein Gev and Ma'agan Mikhael;
– the natural history museums such as Beit Sturman at Ein Harod and Beit Ussishkin on the Dan kibbutz;
– the collection of art and oriental studies of Wilfred Israel on the Hazorea kibbutz.

Contemporary Israeli art
In Israel art blossoms in the streets, in the gardens, beside the sea or in the desert, a tangible reminder of the common

enlightenment of the country; it is a young, contemporary art.

In Tel Aviv it is very pleasant to stroll down Gordon Street and the neighbouring roads where many art galleries have permanent exhibitions, such as the Gordon, Mabbat, Hadassa'K and Yodfat galleries. In the surrounding district, in Bar Yam, Petah Tikva and Ramat Gan, you can find very interesting small modern art museums.

In Jaffa artists paint by day and hold evening shows of their work. This makes night-time walks through the old city's streets, where every painter will welcome you into his booth, a very charming pastime. Several other towns also have artists' quarters – Ein Hod near Haifa (with its important Municipal Museum), Yamin Moshe and Ein Karem, both close to Jerusalem, and Safad where naive painting is well represented.

A great many works by Israeli artists are on display in the museums. The most important are the very modern Tel Aviv museum and sculpture garden and the National Museum of Israel where you must visit the drawing collection. In the Billy Rose Sculpture Gardens on Neve Sha'anan hill you can walk among sculptures of all periods. The synagogue in the Hadassah Medical Centre park contains admirable stained-glass windows by Marc Chagall. The Ein Harod museum near Lake Tiberias collects works by Jewish artists from Israel and the west, besides works by kibbutzim artists.

Art is an integral part of the countryside in the buildings, where sculpture and painting merge with architecture, often mixing the abstract characteristics of the modern vision with the permanence of the age-old biblical faith. In the courtyard of the Tel Aviv law courts there is a low stone representing a scroll in which a chapter of the Pentateuch, the oldest text of the law, is inscribed: the hole pierced through the centre of the stone is a kind of eye which looks at you and through which you can look, intimating that the law is not a one-way process. At Beersheba the Palmach Brigade memorial celebrates the memory of heroes but, at the same time, by integrating light, water and fire, it celebrates life itself.

Gary Bertini. *Born in Russia, he studied composing and conducting in Israel, in Milan and then in Paris under Arthur Honegger. Founder and leader of the Israel Chamber Ensemble and the Rinat choir, he is one of the key figures in Israel's musical life. He is also one of the leaders of the Scottish National Orchestra, the B.B.C. Orchestra and also conducts in Europe and the United States in many concerts and operas.*

Musical events

Israel is mad about music! All year round the country holds musical activities and public participation is, proportionally, the highest in the world.

At Eastertime the Ein Gev festival takes place on the east bank of Lake Tiberias and in May you can listen to sacred Christian music at Abu Gosh.

The Israel festival is held from mid-July to the end of August in the ancient setting of the Caesarea amphitheatre, as well as in Jerusalem and Tel Aviv. The best Israeli orchestras and international musicians and singers appear there.

Authur Rubenstein appears with the Israel Philharmonic Orchestra in a kind of mini-festival at the end of September.

Musical weeks are held around Christmas allowing concert-goers to familiarise themselves with works by composers such as Oedoen Partos, Mordechai Seter, Ben Zion Orgad, Josef Tal, Noam Sheriff, Tzvi Avni.

Throughout the year the Israel Philharmonic Orchestra performs the great classics in 35 appearances in all the important towns and with guest appearances by international conductors and musicians.

The Israel Chamber Orchestra of Tel Aviv is swiftly increasing in popularity, giving public concerts on the kibbutzim and in country villages.

The Israeli Opera, also in Tel Aviv, performs the best-known operas six nights a week. In Jerusalem, on Tuedays, you can go and listen to the public concerts given by the Israeli Radio and Television Symphony Orchestra.

If you go to Haifa you will find that the city has its own symphony orchestra which gives a number of concerts.

Chamber music evenings are held in Holon, Ramat Gan and Haifa.

There are around a 120 choirs which give concerts all over the country with programmes of western music and Israeli folk songs.

The music academies in Tel Aviv and Jerusalem have produced many talented and recognised artists.

As well as being known for its purely musical talent, Israel has also acquired a reputation for choreography with the Yemenite ballet Ynbal and the Batsheva and Bat Dor companies (these last two thanks to the dynamism of the Baroness Batsheva de Rothschild).

Music and dancing are important to the Israeli public and well-known artists such as Leonard Bernstein, Isaac Stern, Theresa Stich Randall, Claudio Arrau, Otto Klemperer, Pablo Casals and Yehudi Menuhin display their talent all year round.

Education in Israel

Education in Israel has three simultaneous objectives:

– it wishes to ensure that Israeli society has a high level of cultural knowledge instilled as much with universal values as with Jewish tradition. As far as the latter is concerned, it intends to pool the spiritual richness of the 80 communities which make up the nation while respecting and allowing their special characters to develop.

– it intends to reduce and progressively erase the different standards among the communities which have come to Israel from parts of the world which differ not only geographically but also socially and culturally.

– it is striving to make the state of Israel attain the level of thought and research and technological capability indispensible for ensuring its development.

Israel is a country which is developing ultra-rapidly. It is also subject to internal and external pressures which are rough and permanent. Planning has constantly been made difficult here not only by the wars endured by the country but also by the irregular and unforeseeable graph of immigration. The setting-up of a system of education which is at the same time culturally advanced, socially fair and effective, presents particularly delicate problems. The results up to now are very encouraging.

Illiteracy is practically non-existent in Israel. More than 850,000 pupils (a third of the total population) currently attend almost 6,000 centres of teaching.

Education is compulsory and free between the ages of five and 16 years. In fact education actually begins from the age of three in private or public kindergartens.

Currently there are 120,000 pupils attending kindergartens; 600,000 pupils at primary schools (this figure is approximately what the total population of Israel numbered when the country was created!); 70,000 young people attending secondary schools; 50,000 students on courses at the universities of Jerusalem, Tel Aviv, Bar-Ilan, Haifa, Rehovot and Beersheba.

There are some 85,000 Arab children in 400 public schools and kindergartens. Of these 30,000 are enrolled in private schools subsidised by religious or other bodies. The Israeli government encourages the development of the Arab languages and culture in these schools. The teaching of the Muslim and the Christian religions is, naturally, unrestricted.

Let me stress the importance of the adult education system. It is made up of institutions offering a high standard of teaching to people who, because of the particular conditions prevailing in Israel, have either taken up a university course after a long break in their education, or started late in life on secondary education (letters, Jewish studies, Hebrew, social science, foreign languages).

In addition more than 100,000 new immigrants have so far followed intensive courses in the Ulpanim where the most modern methods are employed for the rapid teaching of Hebrew.

The whole of Israel is virtually a huge study-workshop. Teaching and culture bind together a people still evolving their own society; aspiring to find their own secure character; offering their very best to the universal heritage.

If a student coming to Israel wishes to immigrate he should approach either the Commission for Admission (Student Office) 6 Hillel Street, Jerusalem or, in the United Kingdom, Kibbutz Desk, Finchley Road, College House, London NW3, who will give him advice and guidance and direct him to an Ulpan with a view to acquiring a knowledge of Hebrew. They will also help him to obtain grants for subsistence, housing or studies. The first condition, though, is a knowledge of Hebrew. There are two sure ways of attaining this:

1. The State Ulpan or one of the 64 kibbutzim Ulpanim: language teaching here lasts for three to six months. On the kibbutzim the day is divided between manual work and study: on the other hand, the student is fed, housed and cared for.

2. A year at university.

The student (who must hold 'A' levels or equivalent qualifications) will then choose between the various teaching methods available:

A. Officially recognised higher teaching establishments:
   The Bar-Ilan University in Ramat Gan;
   the University College in Haifa;
   the Hebrew University in Jerusalem;
   the Haifa Technion (the Israel Institute of Technology);
   the Negev University in Beersheba;
   the Weizmann Science Institute in Rehovot.

B. Academies and Conservatories:
   the Bezalel Art School in Jerusalem;
   the Samuel Rubin Music Academy in Jerusalem;
   the Samuel Rubin Israeli Conservatoire of Music at Tel Aviv University.

C. Teacher Training Schools in Jerusalem, Natanya, Beersheba, Givat Washington.

D. Specialised professional schools

E. Colleges for Jewish studies.

The photographs are from:

Cover photographs taken by: Jean-Noël Reichel (Top) for Jerusalem and Éric Lessing (Magnum) for the Arava Plain / Atlas Photo: p. 39 left / Bruno Barbey (Magnum): p. 90 / Werner Braun: p. 15, 24, 52, 67, 68, 73 (bottom), 74, 77, 80, 82 (top), 95, 101 (left), 101 (bottom right), 102, 110, 132 / Henri Cartier-Bresson (Magnum): p. 19 (left) / Jean-Philippe Charbonnier (Top): p. 22 (left), 22 (right), 23 / Daniel Frank: p. 21 / Léonard Freed (Magnum): p. 65 / Gisèle Freund: p. 87, 98–99, 126 (top) / Marc Garanger: p. 25 (bottom right), 52 (bottom), 61 (right), 83, 84, 117 / Georges Gerstèr (Rapho): 53, 56, 107 / Louis Goldman (Rapho): p. 16 (bottom), 17, 52 (top), 58, 73 (left) / David Harris: p. 20, 25 (top right), 29, 32, 34 (left), 34 (right), 34 (bottom), 35, 36, 38, 40, 43 (left), 43 (right), 44, 45, (right), 46 (bottom), 47 (top left), 47 (top right), 47 (bottom right), 48, 54, 55 (top), 55 (bottom), 60, 63 (bottom), 72, 75, 82 (bottom), 88, 89 (top), 89 (bottom), 92 (top), 92 (bottom), 93 (top left), 93 (top right), 93 (bottom left), 93 (bottom right), 96, 100, 101 (top right), 103, 105, 106, 108 (bottom), 111, 113 (left), 114 (top), 114 (bottom), 122, 123 (top), 123 (bottom), 126 (centre), 127, 128 (left), 129, 135, 143 / Hassia: p. 136, 137, 142, 144 (left), 144 (right), 145 (left), 145 (right), 146 (left), 146 (right), 147 / Léon Herschtritt: p. 85 (left) / Léon Herschtritt (Parimage): p. 65 / Pascal Hinous: p. 108 (top) / Israel Government Press Office: p. 13, 33, 49, 128 (right), 130, 140 / Kay Lawson (Rapho): p. 47 (bottom left) / Charles Lenars: p. 76 (left), 109 / Éric Lessing (Magnum): p. 37, 46 (top), 50, 69, 97, 104, 109, 112, 133 / Bernard Nantet: p. 41, 42, 66, 68 (bottom), 113 (right), 116, 121 (top), 121 (bottom), 126 (bottom), 141 (left), 141 (right), / Léo Nisen: p. 94 (left) / Parimage: p. 14, 28, 91, 131 / Jean-Noel Reichel (top): p. 58, 59, 61 (top left), 61 (top right), 62, 63 (top left), 63 (top right), 63 (centre left), 63 (bottom left), 63 (bottom right), 64, 70, 71, 74 (top), 78, 81, 85 (right) / David Rubinger: p. 19 (right), 25 (left), 27, 31, 39 (right), 45 (left), 56 76 (right) 86, 108 (centre), 118, 119, 120, 138–139, 143 / David Seymour (Magnum): p. 18, 54 / Spiegel (Rapho): p. 79 / Ph. Stray Myster (Israeli Minister of Tourism): p. 30 / Sabine Weiss (Rapho): p. 16 / Jean-Louis Swiners (Rapho): p. 124–125 / Zafrir: p. 26, 94 (right) / the photographs in the appendix are by J. Agor, R. Gal, O. Garros, S. Harris and B. Sullerot.

detailed contents

We would like to thank
the Israeli Minister of Tourism,
the people named and the many friends
who gave us their kind co-operation
in the realising of this book.

First published by the Librairie Hachette 1972
Original text copyright © Librairie Hachette and Société
d'Études et de Publications Économiques 1972

Design by Erwin Spatz

English translation copyright © Kaye & Ward Ltd 1979
First published in Great Britain by Kaye & Ward Ltd
21 New Street, London EC2M 4NT
1979
First published in the USA by Oxford University Press Inc.
200 Madison Avenue, New York, NY 10016
1980

ISBN 0–7182–1005–0 (Great Britain)
ISBN 0–19–520170–1 (USA)
Library of Congress Catalog Card Number 79–88723 (USA)

Typeset by CCC and bound in Great Britain by
William Clowes & Sons Limited, Beccles & London
Printed in Italy by Mondadori, Verona